YOUR OBSOLETE BRAIN

YOUR OBSOLETE BRAIN

Life and Death in the
Age of Superintelligent Machines

Dennis L. Foster

THE LIFE SCIENCE INSTITUTE

Published by The Life Science Institute

ISBN 978-0-692-90002-4

The Life Science Institute
www.lifescienceinstitute.com
email: lifescience@mail.com

CONTENTS

PREFACE

Why You Need to Read this Book

We are entering a period of profound social and technological transition in which developments in Artificial Intelligence (AI) will completely transform civilization as we know it. Unfortunately, the same technology that might solve the planet's most dire problems has also spawned autonomous killing machines and nanorobots capable of spreading lethal viruses indiscriminately.

As superintelligent machines ascend, will they inherit our competitive drives to succeed, exploit, and dominate? Who will be the real masters of future civilizations: humans or machines? In this book, I seek to provide the most likely answers, based on recent breakthroughs and groundbreaking research, to these and other questions about one of the most important human quests of modern times—possibly of all time.

Many of the most respected thinkers of our time believe that artificial intelligence (AI) is a phenomenon to be feared, whereas advocates of super brainy machines envision a world without disease, famine, economic crisis, and global strife, made possible by advanced analytical and decision making powers beyond the scope of human thinking.

Unquestionably, artificial intelligence has the potential for previously unimagined benefits in numerous fields, including medical diagnosis, disease eradication, education, communications, transportation, and economic crisis management. However, our ever-growing overdependence on technology is fraught with the potential for social upheaval and societal collapse.

The promise of AI has reached a feverish pitch among people who describe themselves as visionary futurists, inspiring a growing cult with all the underpinnings of a religion. These enthusiasts envision a future in which machines equal and eventually surpass humans on the evolutionary scale. Others cling to the idea of uploading their minds to sophisticated computers that duplicate all the functions of a biological brain.

These visionary musings, as well as the potential peril of AI-empowered devices one day "waking up" as self-aware beings, have been the subjects of a flurry of books in the last fifteen years, written not by computer scientists or programmers engaged in AI research and deployment, but by philosophy professors, math teachers, pop science reporters, and other laypersons.

This book is not a scientific treatise, textbook, personal opinion piece, or vision of some theoretical future, but a revelation, based on the factual events, developments, and research that explain how AI is affecting and will continue to affect your life, in ways good, bad, ugly, but also beautiful.

AI milestones are literally toppling like dominoes, day by day. Ultimately, the quality of life and the entire fate of everyone who lives on Earth will be forever impacted by artificial intelligence from birth to death—and possibly beyond.

1

WILL THE HUMAN ERA BE ENDED?

AI, Humanity, and the Planet Earth

"We know what we are but know not what we may be."
William Shakespeare

The machine can cure you.

Row after row of textured ceiling tiles pass before your vision as an attendant in a leaf-green gown pushes the gurney along a brightly lit corridor. In a seemingly endless stream, unfamiliar faces peer down at you, some smiling, some anxious, others studious as if examining a laboratory specimen. Traveling through parting double doors, you find yourself lying in a gleaming white room beneath a cluster of circular light fixtures. Cold air wafts over you as the sheet is removed. A woman wearing a cloth mask hurriedly places a rigid plastic mouthpiece over your face and tells you, "Count backward from one hundred." As you start counting, the last thing you see as your consciousness fades is a set of four mechanical arms, each bearing a surgical instrument, hovering over your chest. The arms are guided by a computer, but the surgery will be controlled by a human surgeon sitting at a console 2,000 miles away.

The machine can kill you.

Against a blood red sky, the silhouette of a turret protrudes from an embankment overlooking a sparsely wooded plain. As darkness descends, the turret begins to move. No human can see what the turret sees as its sophisticated sensors sweep the horizon. Its gun is loaded with lethal radioactive bullets that, should they be unleashed, will explode on impact. The turret is programmed for one mission only—to detect, distinguish, and target an enemy soldier whether in daylight or in darkness. No human guidance or assistance is needed. Unlike a human sniper, the autonomous turret never sleeps, always acquires its target, and never misses.

The machine can obsolete you.

When you learned, not from your supervisor but from a news article on the internet, that your company planned to eliminate 2,000 jobs, your first reactions were denial, shock, betrayal, and, eventually, anxiety. You prayed against all odds that you would be among the spared, that your years of loyalty and uncontested competence would count for some-thing.

There was no pink slip or email, only a list of names posted on a bulletin board in the coffee room. You had no reason to suspect, a week later, standing in the long line at the Unemployment Office, that you had been replaced by a machine—

one that is smarter, works faster and more efficiently, and never calls in sick.

The machine can empower you.

Hannah wakes each morning eager for class. Her favorite subjects are astronomy, theoretical physics, Sub Saharan African languages, and the history of education in antiquity. To her, it seems like only yesterday she could barely perform the simplest calculus equation or speak more than a few phrases in Matabele. In fact, it was three months ago. Greeting her tutor, she is ready for an assessment of her knowledge of the behavior of matter/antimatter particle pairs approaching the perimeter of a black hole. To her computer-tutor, Hannah is an average learner, has a tendency to mumble, and is fifteen years old.

If you find these scenarios far-fetched, you need to know that the technologies portrayed in these snippets of some seemingly future world already exist. Artificial Intelligence (AI) can diversely cure, kill, obsolete, or educate in ways previously only imagined.

AI advances in medical diagnosis and treatment have the potential to eradicate diseases that were once considered incurable. Yet, what most disturbs many people about AI research today is the horrific potential to kill, on a scale rivaled only by nuclear weapons. Others are concerned by predictions that robots and other AI-empowered devices will replace half of the world's work force. At the same time, the educational technologies already exist to facilitate, augment, and accelerate learning as never before contemplated.

The specter of autonomous weapons equipped with human reasoning, superintelligent computers disdainful of their intellectually human inferiors, and virus-like nanorobots is more real than most people want to believe. The means to create weapons that operate independently of human operators is easily accessible. From flying laser cannons to robot tanks, development of AI-controlled weapons has already spawned a futuristic arms race.

The Russian Republic rolled out its Armata T-14 fully robot-capable battle tank in August, 2015, the first of a planned fleet of 2,400 such death machines. America has been developing robotic aircraft and ground weapons since the 1970s. In 2016, the U.S. Navy announced its intention to deploy robot ships and submarines. More than 90 nations currently possess autonomous weapons capable of identifying and destroying targets with pinpoint accuracy. It's not by accident that the first electronic "thinking machine" was designed and built specifically to go to war.

Two parallel research fields are currently attempting to duplicate human intelligence. One of these is based on computer software alone and aims to precisely map the human thought process. The other, based on biological research, strives to reconstruct the neural structure of the human brain.

However, the most important merger of humans with machines most likely will occur not between people and robots, but between artificial intelligence and human-engineered organisms. In bioengineering, artificial intelligence is already more crucial to research outcomes than the humans who direct the research—for example, in decoding DNA, designing and altering genes, and mapping brain functions.

The convergence of AI, virtual reality, and neuroscience holds the promise for methodologies to treat autism, attention deficit disorders, depression, and other psychiatric problems, but also for use as erotic stimulation and pornography.

AI is currently used in business environments to mine for data about the purchasing habits and demographics of internet users, formulate marketing plans, provide pseudo-robotic "service agents" on websites, and train workers. Future AI programs may succeed in replacing vast portions of the work force, from marketing and accounting personnel to entire creative and training departments. AI also has the potential to facilitate corporate sabotage, database theft, and fraud.

In some ways comparable to casino gambling, stock market fluctuations are subject to identifiable influences that can be tracked, analyzed, interpreted, and predicted according to logical rules. AI is deployed in investment programs used to make market decisions, and will eventually control entire national and international economies, administered by machines capable of making expert decisions independently of human interference.

The most enthusiastic advocates of artificial intelligence envision a future when super-brainy machines will be capable of independent reasoning, becoming sentient beings with all the mental faculties of humans but vastly superior in intelligence. These enthusiasts refer to their vision as the Singularity, based on a science fiction novel by a writer named Verne Vigne.

“Within 30 years, we will have the technological means to create superhuman intelligence,” Vinge predicted in 1993. “Shortly after, the human era will be ended.” That event Vinge termed "the Singularity," a point when, in his view, sentient computers will transform society and eventually dominate every aspect of human existence.

Vigne's musings inspired an enthusiastic cult of science fiction fans, self-styled visionary futurists, pop science writers, and philosophy professors—a cult that has grown in proportion to a metaphysical belief system.

Other Singularity proponents dream of extremely sophisticated neural computer networks capable of housing the mind of a human being. The premise for this cyber dream is based on the notion that at some point computers will be capable of creating their own updates and enhancements, enabling them to design even more advanced computers. Eventually, the more advanced computers would spawn even brainier machines, and so on, eventuating in the creation of an exact neural replica of the human brain.

All these present and emerging envisionings, including the notion of a technological Singularity, are explored in depth in the following chapters. The question that most haunts researchers, mathematicians, and college professors today also begs answering: Disdainful of human limitations, will the AI-controlled machines of the future turn against their inventors and indiscriminately destroy human civilization?

A NASA-funded study has predicted the probability of "the complete collapse of civilization as we know it" before the year 2050. Theoretical physicist Stephen Hawking has forecast the end of humankind within 100 years. Ceding the possibility that humans by themselves are incapable of solving and managing the many threats to their existence from global climate change, overpopulation, famine, disease, and war, artificial intelligence may hold the best promise of human survival.

However, dwindling global resources and shrinking sustainability threaten to derail not just the quest for machines that can reason, but civilization itself. Ordinary planetary and astronomical influences are also serious perils to both existing and future integration of technology. Solar storms, magnetic field disruptions, rising oceans, and geological disturbances have the capacity to disrupt and even extinguish the global power grid, instantly transforming every electrical device on earth into useless junk. The level of preparedness of nations and organizations for such catastrophes is at best a token effort.

As surely as climate change, global terrorism, famine, and disease threaten the survival of humanity and civilization, no survival blueprint for the future of governments, corporations, organizations, and individuals can afford to ignore the potentially devastating social, industrial, and military impacts of the rapidly dawning Age of Superintelligent Machines.

The Quest for Superintelligence

The quest for super brainy, independently reasoning computers has never been more fervent. In recent decades, AI systems have been explored and implemented, with varying degrees of success, at virtually every level of business, education, and government, from financial services and manufacturing to national defense. However, to duplicate even the most miniscule component of a human brain's cognitive function would require vast resources presently beyond the means of any government or enterprise.

Theoretically, given sufficient resources, it would be possible using existing technology to create a thinking machine with exactly the same neural functions as a human biological brain, with computer chips acting as "neurons" and "memory cells." These "neurons" and "memory cells" could be made to send and receive the same types of electrical impulses that constitute human cognition and memory. However, this feat by itself would hardly ensure that human-like self-awareness and experience would be possible. In fact, new research has upended everything neuroscientists have believed about neurons and memory previously.

Your brain has more than 100 billion neurons and 1,000 trillion synaptic connections. It constantly receives sensory data and processes information at speeds far beyond that of even the most advanced computer.

A rich memory such as an event involving interaction with other people, recognition of a face, the scent of a flower, colors, not to mention facts learned, books read, movies watched, even Twitter tweets and Facebook likes, involves numerous parts of the brain working in concert. A single human memory composed and stored in a ribbon of protein inside a brain cell can be recalled in less than a nanosecond, sometimes with missing or altered details but sometimes also with near-perfect retention. Amazingly, recent experiments have shown that simple memories can be erased from the brain cells in which they are stored and yet resurrected later.

It cannot be dismissed that a human mind may not be analogous to computer software at all. There may be no algorithm, architecture, or blueprint for the rich tapestry of human experience, much less for awareness. To use Plato's metaphor, computer memories may prove to be mere "shadows on the cave wall," a soul-less representation of the reality that humans experience.

Some AI enthusiasts have expressed the opinion that, perhaps as soon as thirty years from now, supercomputers will be capable of creating their own software updates, designing and manufacturing enhanced versions of themselves, and eventually spawning something resembling an independently reasoning artificial brain, vastly more efficient than the combined brain power of all humans who were ever born.

Civilization currently faces a mind-boggling array of challenges which may be beyond the ability of humans to meet successfully without the aid of intelligent machines: disease, famine, poverty, climate change, and the rapidly accelerating extinction of species, to name a few.

There is no lack of media space devoted to sensationalist fears about the threat of super intelligent computers gone mad. Yet, in truth, artificial intelligence may be best hope for the long-term survival of both humankind and the planet.

Viewed in the light of current scientific knowledge, a truly sentient machine, whether a computer, network, robot, or weapon, is largely a fantasy and may continue to be so until the extinction of our own species. Nevertheless, the quest for superintelligent machines holds the promise of immense impact on medical diagnosis and disease eradication, economic crisis management, and, inevitably, military resources required to fight terrorism and defend against invasion.

Can We, Should We, Will We?

Skeptics have a legitimate fear that equipping weaponry with independent reasoning will spawn an AI weapons arms race. However, beyond expert systems and machine-engineered updates, new research in "deep learning" aims to make use of artificial neural networks, similar to the architecture of the human brain. Such networks theoretically could process complicated concepts, such as how to eradicate disease, poverty, and famine, or reverse global climate change, more efficiently and accurately than any team or organization composed of humans alone.

Eventually, superintelligent machines will transport people and goods, diagnose and treat diseases, and protect personal assets from financial crises.

Some things you might not have imagined include computers that can synthesize human DNA, create new vaccines, perform surgery, and formulate new wonder drugs;

machines that seed and plow fields, manage farms, and distribute produce to market; devices that monitor, analyze, and manage entire economies; prevent stock market crashes and financial malpractice by banks; computers that teach, evaluate, and challenge learners with the benefit of the combined knowledge of the most advanced minds of all humankind.

Such machines may seem to be the stuff of science fiction, yet someday they will become an integral part of your life and the lives of everyone who lives after you.

As you will discover in the following chapters, recent AI breakthroughs hold the promise to greatly enhance the quality of life of present and future generations, and to assist in solving dire global problems.

Yet it should not be ignored that the AI arms race is already underway, and it may be too late to prevent thinking-machine chaos. Autonomous weapons already awaiting deployment and currently on the drawing boards, if perverted by terrorists and rogue nations, realistically could wreak mass destruction on a scale surpassing Hiroshima.

AI also threatens to make humans in virtually every walk of life obsolete, creating not the utopia of universal comfort and wealth we seek, but a dystopia of poverty, discontent, and social upheaval.

It is too late to ask: can we, should we, will we? The superintelligent machine, able to think like a human, but vastly more knowledgeable than any or all of us together, is coming—whether you're ready or not.

Global Prevalence of AI by Category

Military/Autonomous weapons	32%
Medicine/Health care	20%
Business/Industry	18%
Entertainment/Leisure	12%
Education/Training	10%
Science/Research	8%

2

OPEN THE POD BAY DOOR, PLEASE

The Lore and Loathing of Super Computers

"Fantasy, abandoned by reason, produces impossible monsters."
Francisco de Goya

When philosophers and scientists first began dreaming about thinking machines, few people feared, loathed, or resented the idea. Precisely the opposite, most people were excited about the possibilities.

Humanity has dreamed of wisdom-spouting constructs since ancient times. Built at least 10,000 years ago, the limestone statue of the Great Sphinx guarding the Pyramids of Giza was said to communicate with humans telepathically. In the King's Chamber located at the end of an underground tunnel beneath the statue, Napoleon Bonaparte claimed to have had a vision foretelling his eventual demise.

Though ancient mythology is sprinkled with animated statues and magical furniture (none of which were alleged to possess sentient qualities), the idea of a machine created by humans and capable of independent reasoning was beyond the grasp of ancient philosophers and kings.

No sooner did computers enter the public consciousness than fantasy, abandoned by reason—or augmented by fear—began producing impossible monsters.

Impossible Monsters of Film

In America, the Golden Age of Cinema of the 1950s revolutionized entertainment of the masses. What could be more sensational than the notion that someday humans would be imperiled by computers more intelligent and powerful than humanity itself?

The first cinematic glimpse of the evils of superintelligent computers was provided as early as 1956 in *Forbidden Planet*, a futuristic retelling of Shakespeare's play, *Tempest*. Central to the plot is a huge computer complex powered by 9,200 thermonuclear reactors, which has become fused with the intellect of its caretaker, Professor Morbius (played by former silent film star Walter Pidgeon). Human visitors are imperiled by invisible monsters from the professor's id—the dark component of the human psyche that demands immediate gratification of needs, uninfluenced by moral or ethical sensibilities.

Ten years later, the Cold War-inspired *Colossus: the Forbin Project*, based on a 1966 novel by D. F. Jones, portrayed a collusion between identical U.S. and Soviet super computers, created to control their nations' respective nuclear missile arsenals. The intent was to take over the world and impose a new order on mankind "for its own good." (The film's leading man, Eric Braeden, went on to become one of the most popular Soap Opera characters of all time, Victor

Neuman, in the CBS series *The Young and the Restless.*) In the film's conclusion, the triumphant computer announces to humanity, "In time you will come to regard me with not only awe and respect, but love." Ever since, intelligent machines as villains have become ingrained in popular culture.

No words spoken between a human and a machine in a cinematic event have become more recognizable than these:

Dave: "Open the pod bay doors, please, HAL."

HAL: "I'm sorry, Dave, I can't do that."

This iconic dialog from the highly acclaimed motion picture *2001: A Space Odyssey* and its plot of a rogue computer driven to murder by its intrinsic will to survive succinctly express the apprehension felt by society and many of its finest minds toward the notion of superintelligent machines. The thinking goes something like this: Make a machine that can think like a human and it will behave like a human, but without morality or ethics—or, more precisely, like a human without morality or ethics. In other words, a psychopath.

In theaters across America, as Dave the astronaut, deprived of re-entry to his spaceship home by its intransigent sentient computer, was sent spinning off into the vacuum of space to an eerie silence, the audience also became eerily silent, emotionally jolted by the event.

Fearing that the astronauts were ready to disable it as a result of a supposed diagnostic error, HAL, the *Heuristically programmed ALgorithmic* computer in control of the spacecraft, simply put, suffered a mental breakdown. The critically heralded and gloriously cinematographed film was based on a novel by a science fiction author of considerable notoriety, Arthur C. Clarke. His message was clear: A machine given human intelligence would be subject to human frailties, including mental disease. Yet, HAL was not intrinsically evil, but merely following the dictates of his human-engineered programming to survive at all costs, by whatever means at its disposal, in order to complete its mission.

Human soldiers, in fact, do no less.

From the original *Star Trek* TV series to the *Matrix* movies, humans and independently reasoning machines have battled for decades for supremacy in fictional portrayals of the potential threat of artificial intelligence.

Perhaps the most disturbing super machine of all was the Proteus IV computer in the 1977 film *Demon Seed.* The inventor, named Alex Harris, announces the machine's birth in the following words:

> *This morning, at exactly 5:18 a. m. here at ICON's Institute for Data Analysis we installed the final module on the artificial intelligence system which we call Proteus Four. Today a new dimension has been added to the concept of the computer. Today Proteus Four will begin to think. And it will think with a power and a precision that will make obsolete many of the functions of the human brain.*

The most ominous and prophetic words of this fictional tirade are these: "... make obsolete many of the functions of the human brain." Such words constitute the very premise that many academics today fear and loathe. As the human brain becomes obsolete, how will we even be able to communicate with superintelligent machines, anticipate their behavior, and compete with them for survival? Indeed, it might be argued that the computers of today have already made obsolete many functions of the human brain.

In *Demon Seed*, the character Alex Harris leaves his wife Susan, memorably played by Oscar-winning actress Julie Christie, with the supposed intent of conducting independent research. Proteus IV takes control of every aspect of her life and eventually tortures, rapes, and impregnates her, acting out the machine's quest to obtain humanity.

In the pivotal scene, Julie Christie's character desperately inquires of the computer: "Why must you have a child?" Proteus responds:

> *"Why? So that I may be complete. My intelligence alive in human flesh touching the universe, feeling it. You have named this process "evolution". I am a machine that offered men the triumph of reason and they rejected it. My child will not be so easily ignored. But this child is the world's hope."*

"Then there's no hope, " Susan Harris replies. "I'd rather die."

Before *Space Odyssey* and *Demon Seed*, the Starship Enterprise, the iconic exploratory space vehicle in the *Star Trek* television series, was "infected" by an artificial intelligence virus threatening the existence of humanity. Though clearly perilous to the human crew, to the logic-oriented alien science officer, Mr. Spock, the machine's justification for eradicating the inferior human presence was "entirely logical." Indeed, what could be more logical than cleansing the universe of the most invasive, polluting, infective, deleterious organism ever to emerge from a primordial ooze? Beyond doubt, any independently reasoning super machine would reach the same conclusion.

How, then, do designers of superintelligent computers merge human moral and ethical values with those of the machine? The answer may not be as simple as the question.

The most elaborate "Fear the Machine" culture was devised for the *Matrix* film series, in which the entire human species is portrayed as a fuel source controlled by sentient machines. In the *Matrix* dystopia, humans are grown and nourished in a network of laboratory pods as a source for bioelectricity and thermal energy, their minds controlled by cybernetic implants connecting them to a simulated reality called the Matrix.

Impossible Monsters of Literature

In literature, probably the earliest fictional depiction of a mechanical device possessing human-like intelligence was imagined by L. Frank Baum in the children's story *Ozma of Oz.* A mechanical man dubbed Tik-Tok utilized separate clock-work springs devoted to thinking, action, and speech.

To cite the prevalence of AI in science fiction literature would constitute a virtual litany of superintelligent computers, anthropomorphic robots, sensient holograms, and autonomous spacecraft, both good and evil. One literary portrayal, however, is noteworthy for its role not in a work of science fiction, but in an intellectual adventure story by Umberto Eco, one of the most brilliant novelists and thinkers of the modern era. In *Foucault's Pendulum*, a satire on the futility of conspiracy theories and those who believe them, a personal computer called Abulafia is used to reorganize random words using "if-then" rules to generate conspiracy theories, secret plans, and solutions to abstruse puzzles involving the Knights Templar, secret codes, and the overthrow of all the world's governments. Though Eco never divulged the name's origin, most likely his fictional prophetic computer was named after a real person, Abraham Abulafia, a 13th-Century self-styled prophet and messiah, who wrote several books and poems devoted to extreme forms of mystical experiences.

The story describes the plight of three book editors who, inspired by a bizarre conspiracy story, input random bits of information into the computer, believing they are only playing a game. When the game begins to merge with reality, the deaths begin to mount, and they are forced into a frantic search to decipher the true meaning of the game.

The author's premise is succinctly expressed in this conclusion by one of the characters:

> *"I have come to believe that the whole world is an enigma, a harmless enigma that is made terrible by our own mad attempt to interpret it as though it had an underlying truth."*

Verne Vigne, despite his present-day notoriety among Singularity devotees, as a science fiction writer never achieved the popularity or acclaim of Kurt Vonnegut, Robert Heinlein, or Arthur C. Clarke, the most famous authors of the genre.

Player Piano, Vonnegut's first novel, published in 1952, is regarded by many devotees of the genre as a defining moment in AI science fiction. The novel depicts a dystopian post-World War III future populated by machines that have functionally replaced virtually all human workers, creating an insurmountable disparity in wealth between the technology-controlling upper class and the obsoleted lower class.

To Vonnegut, the player piano is a metaphor representing how even a simple activity, such as teaching oneself to play the piano, can be replaced by a machine.

In a 1973 interview, the author explained:

> "Player Piano *was my response to the implica-ions of having everything run by little boxes...To have a little clicking box make all the decisions wasn't a vicious thing to do. But it was too bad for the human beings who got their dignity from their jobs."*

In 1968, Robert Heinlein wrote *The Moon is a Harsh Mistress*, featuring the High Optical, Logical Multi-Evaluating Supervisor (HOLMES IV) computer. Its designers continued augmenting its powers until it became self-aware and began taking an interest in humor and pranks. The story is about the friendship between HOLMES and a Russian-born engineer Manuel O'Kelly, or "Man" for short, who lead a rebellion on the moon, which has become a dumping ground for Earth's criminals.

In his story, Heinlein predicted the premise and power of data mining:

> *"There is no worse tyranny than to force a man to pay for what he does not want merely because you think it would be good for him."*

Impossible Monsters of College Professors

Riding the anti-AI hysteria popularized by entertainment media, Oxford philosophy professor Nick Bostrom penned *Superintelligence: Paths, Dangers, Strategies*, envisioning a world in which a superintelligent machine could be programmed, for example, to make paper clips.

> *Maybe it would want to get rid of humans, so we don't switch it off, because then there would be fewer paper clips. Human bodies consist of a lot of atoms and they can be used to build more paper clips.*

Bostrom, a Swede, foresees not a gradual, methodical advancement but a super-fast leap from beneficent artificial intelligence to the rise of sentient, potentially evil, independently reasoning super machines:

> *I don't think that the artificial-intelligence train will slow down or stop at the human-ability station. Rather, it's likely to swoosh right by it... we might go, in a relatively brief period of time, from something slightly sub-human to something radically superintelligent.*

"Swoosh" isn't an actual word, but Bostrom was apparently referring to the sound of a subway train racing past a crowd of disbelieving people waiting at a station (in this case, the "human-ability station").

We are now at the point where the impossible monsters imagined by science fiction, mainstream cinema, and philosophy professors are nearing realization. The notion that some future computer could suddenly "wake up" as a fully sentient being and decide to enslave humanity or make humans into paper clips may seem far-fetched, but the horrific peril presented by autonomous weapons and virus-like nanorobots is only too real.

The problem is that no weapon ever invented, no matter how heinous, has "not been used." In the words of astronomer

Stephen Galloway, "a weapon is a manifestation of a preconceived notion." Weapons are created for the specific purpose of killing, destructing, or disrupting. Furthermore, no invention, once realized, can be "uninvented." There is no reason to believe the experience will be different with autonomous killing machines. Nevertheless, it is necessary to conceive of a weapon in order to defend against it.

At least 90 countries across the globe are currently stocking up on AI weapons, anticipating the time when machines alone, without human direction, will make the decision as to whom, when, and how to kill.

The challenge of programming AI weapons with ethical sensibilities to prevent killing-machine chaos is daunting. For one thing, software can be altered, corrupted, replaced, or deleted, transforming the presumably ethical battlebot into a marauding mechanical terrorist.

A second problem is the subjective nature of ethics; one person's moral code is another person's sign of weakness. Though most people may agree that creating an intelligent machine capable of killing innocent men, women, and children indiscriminately would violate some common standard of human decency, there are, unfortunately, humans who consider that their own beliefs or causes justify any means.

Ultimately, it's the not the rise of robots that we need to fear; it's the vestige of the killer instinct still lingering in *Homo Sapiens*.

3

AN ANIMAL IN THE CAVE

How to Make a Thinking Machine

"The real problem is not whether machines think, but whether men do."
B.F. Skinner

Computers were not designed to reason about the world or contemplate the meaning of life. The first computational devices were created to solve math equations, sort through data, and perform such tasks as determining where to point artillery to achieve the most accuracy. Ironically, when handheld calculators came into vogue in the 1970s, each such device was more powerful and efficient than the room-sized computers of only a decade earlier.

The modern counterpart to the Greek oracles, the AI rule-based system, was a near fulfillment of the ages old dream of an advice-spewing construct. A machine equipped with AI offers worldly advice and recommendations by mimicking the way we solve problems.

As an example, a conventional computer program can perform calculations and process text typed on a keyboard. In contrast, an AI program tests various hypotheses to determine if they are correct or false, in order to form a conclusion. In essence, it's the same way a human forms conclusions.

A simple computer program used for medical diagnosis coughs up information from a database of diseases, symptoms, and treatments. An AI program queries the consulting physician about the patient's symptoms and lab results, analyzes images, and then makes a recommendation on how to proceed with a cure.

The Logical Distinction

If you want to understand the science behind machine reasoning, you need to know something about the study of human logic. Thinking machines were made possible by navel-gazing philosophers who spent the better part of their time contemplating their own ability to contemplate, reaching back to ancient Greece. In this day and age, it may seem strange that the smartest people once spent their waking hours pondering over the question of how and why we think. Yet, thanks to that very preoccupation, science was created and, with it, the eventual development of thinking machines. Today, more than ever, exploring the nature of human reasoning has become essential to further advancement in artificial intelligence.

What most distinctively separates humans from other animals is our capacity for logic. That capacity isn't a magic trick. Our brains are structured in such a way that we can analyze and solve apparent quandaries by thinking the problems through. Basically, logic consists of recognition of cause-effect relationships in nature: "If this happens, then that will certainly happen." The end result of logical analysis is a decision of some sort.

On an elementary level, such analysis might take the form of something as simple as "If I am driving on the freeway and there is an accident up ahead, then I will become stuck in traffic." Your decision might be to take the next turnoff onto a side street to bypass the traffic jam. This type of instant "if/then" shortcut is called heuristic reasoning.

On a more sophisticated level, a physician may detect that a patient's EKG has a particular pattern characterized by a jump between two parts called the S wave and the T wave. Upon testing, the patient's blood is found to contain elevated levels of a substance known as SGOT. The physician, therefore, concludes the patient has suffered a myocardial infarction—a heart attack. This scenario is also an example of heuristic reasoning.

We all exercise heuristic reasoning in our daily lives, and all logic can be reduced to such "if/then" rules.

> *"If the sun has risen, and it is not Saturday or Sunday, then I need to get out of bed and get dressed for work."*
>
> *"If there is an animal in my bedroom and it is barking, it is my pet dog Barky."*
>
> *"If my boss tells a joke, then I will laugh (even if it's not funny)."*

Of course, such heuristics seem trivial by comparison to those of early Homo Sapiens:

> *"If the sun has risen, I need to leave the cave and hunt for food."*

> *"If there is an animal in my cave and it is growling, I will be eaten."*

Indeed, such rules are known formally as "shallow reasoning." Virtually all human expertise can be reduced to shallow reasoning, using heuristic shortcuts, thus bypassing what might otherwise be a tedious and time-consuming exercise.

For example, it is enough to know that if a patient's EKG result depicts an elevated S-T segment, and his blood test results indicate a high level of SGOT, he has experienced a heart attack. Why? Because these two findings virtually never occur together except after a heart attack. Such shallow reasoning is the basis for the science of heuristics.

Other animals besides humans might seem to exercise logic at times; for example, when a cheetah evaluates a herd of wildebeest before deciding how and which one to attack, or when the lead goose of a flock in flight traces a transoceanic route to their mating grounds using landmarks as a guide.

In such animals, actions that we humans might perceive as decisions are made on the basis of stimulus-response relationships. For every stimulus, there is an exact and predictable response, from the simplest particles that make up all matter to the most complex organisms.

The human capacity for logic is neither more nor less than an extremely sophisticated expression of the stimulus-response mechanism shared by all matter and life forms.

The Origins of Inference

After acquiring the capacity for logic, it took our predecessors quite a long time to start documenting it. Homo Sapiens has been around for about 195,000 years, but the first written rules of logic didn't occur until the fifth century BC—or 194,500 years later. Aristotle was one of the first thinkers who attempted to lay out a system of logical rules to use in philosophical arguments. Philosophy was a major preoccupation at the time, because there was little in the way of science or physics to challenge intellectuals. Yet, the people who lived then had identical mental capabilities as we do now. Philosophy, speculating about the nature of reality, became their obsession.

Aristotle's teacher was Plato, generally regarded today as the "father of philosophy," who devoted most of his adult life to the art of logical argument.

The platform for Aristotle's system of logic is the concept of *syllogismos*, or deduction. He defined deduction as a statement or argument consisting of a premise that results in a conclusion. More specifically, the premise (*protasis* in Greek) must "necessarily result" in the conclusion (*superasma*). He divided all arguments into two types: deduction and induction.

In college philosophy classes today, the word syllogism still refers to statements in which the conclusions directly follow from their premises. Consider, for example, this argument:

> *"If an animal has wings and can fly, and if it is not an insect or mammal, it is a bird."*

The premises are that the animal has wings, it can fly, and it is not an insect or mammal. The conclusion that follows is that the animal must be a bird. If any one of the premises is false, the conclusion is false. For example, bats, which are mammals, have wings and can fly, but are not birds. Flying fish are animals that can fly, and are not insects or mammals, but they don't have wings.

A statement in which the conclusion is not supported by its premises is known, not surprisingly, as an invalid syllogism.

Another way of looking at a syllogism is as a sentence that can be either true or false, i.e., an assertion. In Aristotle's definition, all assertions must contain a subject and a predicate, and must be demonstrably true or false. The subject and predicate are referred to as the terms of the assertion.

Here is a modern-day example: "If interest rates rise, real estate sales will decline." The subjects are "interest rates" and "real estate sales." The predicates are "rise" and "decline." Note that the subjects are individual, whereas the predicates are general or universal concepts.

Aristotle defined a demonstration as a "deduction that creates knowledge". This concept formed the basis for scientific investigation.

Assertions that are in direct opposition to one another form a contradiction; for example:

1. Interest rates will rise.
2. Interest rates will decline.

These two events cannot occur simultaneously. Only one of these sentences can be true, and, thus, the other must be false. If interest rates rise, it is not possible that they will decline at the same time.

As scientific investigation evolved, recognizing contradictions was crucial to discovery, as is evident in this example:

1. The earth revolves around the sun.
2. The sun revolves around the earth.

Boldly Leaping From the Known to the Unknown

Logic was a favorite theme of the French philosopher Rene Descartes, best known for the mantra "I think, therefore I am". It was he who first put forth the notion that empirical knowledge might be deduced with the same degree of certainty as mathematical theorems. His scheme, "methodological skepticism," was based on the elimination of variable hypotheses through systematic doubt—in other words, testing theories from the standpoint of their possible falsehood rather than their truth. This notion is the model on which the system of investigation used by AI programs is based.

Of all the theorists whose writings inspired the development of machine thinking, perhaps John Dewey, an eminent philosopher, geologist, and educator, can be said to be the most influential. Dewey viewed logic not as an academic exercise but as a concrete method of inquiry to be applied to human problems. He wrote:

> *The process of arriving at an idea of what is absent on the basis of what is at hand is called inference. Every inference, just because it goes beyond the ascertained and known facts, which are either given by observation or by recollection of prior knowledge, involves a jump from the known into the unknown.*

Dewey further stressed the necessity of validating inference and distinguishing between empirical cause-effect relationships and predictive ones. "What is important," he contended, "is that every inference be a tested inference." In these three statements, he effectively described the basis for all modern artificial intelligence programs.

The logic deployed in developing artificial intelligence is derived directly from the navel-gazing system set forth by Aristotle and later refined by Thomas Dewey. Numerous other philosophers devoted their lives to creating mathematical representations of logical analysis, exploring its semantic aspects, and indulging in metaphysics based on intuition as opposed to scientific knowledge. When at last it came time to equip a machine with the ability to solve problems by mimicking human reasoning, it was the musings of Aristotle and Dewey that were most easily applied in the language of Xs and Os that constitute the basis of a machine's processing of instructions and data.

No machine, of course, is aware that it even exists; its only knowledge about itself consists of data that has been input by a human or acquired from analyzing its surroundings. Unlike humans, toddling computers do not lie in a fragrant meadow and gaze upward at the sky, filled with wonder.

Artificial intelligence consists of programming that follows human rules of logic. The program tests each premise that is presented to it to determine if the premise is true or false. If it is true, the premise becomes a fact and leads to the testing of other premises. If the premise is false, the program leaps backward and begins testing an alternative premise. This event is called reiteration.

For example, consider a program designed to defend a nation against a nuclear attack. Assume an image captured by a satellite depicts numerous objects in flight on a trajectory toward the nation's borders. The software first tests to see if the objects match images of known transcontinental missiles. If the images do not match, the program backtracks and tests if the objects resemble known fighting aircraft. If the images still fail to match, the program tests further for geese, ducks, ice crystals, or whatever else is in its database, before deciding whether to launch a counter attack (or recommend an increase in the price of poultry futures on the Commodities Exchange.)

However, not all logic is absolute. In terms of how humans perceive reality, the rules of logic often have not one but multiple possible conclusions, with various shades in between. Consider this question Mae West once posed to W. C. Fields:

> *"Is that a gun in your pants, or are you just glad to see me?"*

Expressed as rule-based logic, the proposition would go something like this:

1. If that is a gun in your pants, you are not glad to see me.

2. If that is not a gun in your pants, you are glad to see me.

However, as humans we instantly, without thinking about it, glean much more from this scenario—for example:

1. If that is not a gun in your pants, it might be a roll of coins.

2. If it is a roll of coins, you are on your way to the bank.

3. If you are on your way to the bank, you are not glad to see me.

4. If neither applies, you are glad to see me.

In this particular scenario, numerous other nuances would also come into play, requiring experience in the perception and visualization of shapes, intuition regarding psychic intent, and recognition of sexuality-related behavior. In the past, this sort of instant recognition based on intuition was beyond the ability of even the most advanced computational devices.

Fuzzy and Fuzzier

To tackle the challenge of forming conclusions based on complex multiform variables, "fuzzy logic" was created, referring not to ducklings, peaches, or bears, but to the slang term for poor TV reception. In fuzzy logic, conclusions to logical propositions may vary based on perception. Probability factors are applied to determine the relative importance of each possible outcome.

Fuzzy logic is based on a theory developed in 1965 by Lotfali Askar Zadeh, better known as Lotfi A. Zadeh, a math professor at the University of California at Berkeley. Zadeh was born in Azerbaijan, which was then part of the Soviet Union, to an Iranian father and a Russian Jewish mother, possibly explaining his use of a "street" term to describe his theory. Logic students today ponder a complete repertoire of so-named fuzzy concepts, from fuzzy numbers and fuzzy algorithms to fuzzy events and fuzzy information.

The objective of fuzzy logic programming is to identify variations in the possible outcome of a proposition, such as visual characteristics of a human face or animal, or shades of different colors. Once fuzzy relationships are defined, it becomes possible to develop fuzzy relational databases. The idea is to enable a software program to handle issues of uncertainty outside the realm of normal logic.

In recent years, applications of fuzzy logic have become widespread, ranging from cameras, camcorders, and washing machines, to industrial process controls, medical instrumentation, and consumer credit processing. Speech and visual recognition programs use fuzzy logic to interpret audible commands and identify objects captured by video input. To determine whether W. C. Fields was indeed glad to see Mae West would require complex fuzzy logic programming with access to a database of hundreds of thousands of visual images as well as scientific data about human sexuality, social mores, and casual conversation.

Speech recognition, natural language processing, and vision processing are applications of tremendous interest, yet, from a programming standpoint, are tedious and complex. A promising solution to the challenge is deep learning.

Deep learning makes use of artificial neural networks, inspired by the architecture of the human brain. The brain's network of over 100 billion neurons and synapses is incredibly efficient and incomparably adept. An artificial neural network uses processors as "neurons" and circuits as "synapses" to process data, presumably in a manner similar to the way the circuitry in our brains works, enabling the computer to learn new information on its own.

The more data that is available to the software, the more useful and accurate its behavior. Providing the computer with the ability to assimilate data on its own, and not only by human input, is essential to an effective AI solution, be it predicting the track of hurricanes, managing crops, or curing diseases.

Or whether it's a gun in someone's pants.

Types of Algorithms

Backtracking
Tests a hypothesis for validity and backtracks if a solution is not confirmed, until the eventual solution is produced.

Branch and Bound
Pursues solutions in the form of a tree, in which subproblems represent branches of the primary problem.

Brute Force
Begins processing at a random point and iterates through every possibility until a solution is produced.

Dynamic Programming
Capable of remembering previous outcomes and results, for use in processing new hypotheses.

Greedy
Designed not just to solve problems, but to arrive at the ideal solution for any given problem.

Parallel
Using parallel processors, pursues multiple solutions simultaneously.

Randomized
Uses a random number at any point during its processing of hypotheses.

Recursive
Attempts to produce a direct solution immediately, then backtracks to find a simpler solution.

Serial
Performs each logic operation in a predefined order.

4

ELEMENTARY, MY DEAR WATSON

How the Past is Changing Your Future

Tears come from the heart and not from the brain.
Leonardo da Vinci

Computers don't weep and never will; for, they will never be capable of experiencing friendship or endearment, nor all the posturing and heartbreak that accompany emotional attachment.

It's said repeatedly that technology will transform society. In reality, society has already been transformed by technology, in ways previously unimagined. Leonardo Da Vinci envisioned flying machines and mechanical statues with moving parts, but he never devoted a single thought to the idea of a machine that would one day rival the human intellect, in work, play, or artistic endeavor.

To understand where artificial intelligence is going and how it will affect human society in the future, you need to know where it has been and how it has already influenced us.

Arising from agriculture, civilization was transformed in the nineteenth century by manufacturing and transportation. Since the turn of the twentieth century, technology, from the telegraph to the smart phone, altered virtually every aspect of human existence. Nevertheless, the unvarying constant in all societal transformation has always been, and always will be, human behavior.

When automobiles first appeared on carriage ways as competition for horse driven buggies, the noisy, smoke-spouting nuisances were viewed as vulgar and intrusive. When telephones came into vogue in the nineteenth century, people actually dressed up for phone calls, as if being improperly dressed while talking to another person, even when unseen, was somehow disgraceful. Today, there are more mobile phones than people in the world. It's not unthinkable, though perhaps still vulgar, to encounter people talking on their phones in restrooms, or to converse by voice or text with a caller who is actually sitting on a toilet.

Calculate or Reason?

Though the controversy over machines that mimic human reasoning may seem relatively new, the notion of a mechanical device to make human-like judgments actually has its roots in the 1930s. When engineers began laying plans for the first electronic "thinking machines," the question arose whether the proposed devices should perform calculations or mimic human reasoning. However, at the time, military applications were more pressing, and interest in the development of AI fell by the wayside.

The biggest believer in the "reasoning machine" school was British academician Alan Turing, who in 1950 published an article putting forth a principle that has become known as the Turing Test. According to this principle, if a machine could carry on a conversation using a teleprinter, indistinguishable from a conversation with a human, it would be reasonable to say that the machine was "thinking."

Though naive from a neurological standpoint, the so-called Turing Test is considered a landmark in the scientific acceptance of the possibility of engineered intelligence. Turing's theory of computation showed that calculations, as well as information, could be described digitally. Research in neurology had shown that the human brain is an electrochemical network, composed of electrically sensitive nerve cells called neurons, that fire intermittently. The coupling of these ideas suggested that it might be possible to construct an electronic brain.

Decades later, as declining hardware costs made information technology more widely available, research teams in both academic and commercial environments began to express renewed interest in Turing's hypotheses.

At the Massachusetts Institute of Technology and Stanford University, researchers speculated about methods of mechanically duplicating human cognition, spawning the term "artificial intelligence" (AI) in 1956. But until the 1960s, the idea of a machine capable of human-like reasoning remained just a theory.

Important conceptual groundwork was laid out at Carnegie Mellon University by Alan Newell and Herbert Simon, who set out to map the processes that underlie the way humans solve problems. The program they produced was called the General Problem Solver (GPS), the first AI program to use something resembling rules of logic. As its name implied, GPS was intended to solve nearly any generalized problem.

The program's designers were seeking a powerful all-in-one algorithm capable of solving any problem, whether in chemistry, math, or language processing. The only requirements, theoretically, were the statement of the goal to be achieved and the rules for processing the goal. Unlike traditional computer programs, GPS was designed to analyze solve different kinds of problems using the same "reasoning" mechanism in every instance. To accomplish this feat, the authors created a new language, called IPL (Information Processing Language). By modern standards, GPS and IPL were very limited as to the types and difficulty of problems they could actually solve.

Studying how humans solve problems, Newell and Simon recognized that we often make decisions based on "means-end" analysis—that is, by defining the means required to achieve a specific end. For example, to arrive at work on time, a person has to travel a certain distance, the means for which is an automobile. If the automobile's battery is dead, the battery will have to be replaced. If there is a traffic jam on the freeway, an alternate route must be taken.

Means-end analysis, as viewed by GPS, involves three components: a goal, preconditions to the goal, and operators (the "means") for facilitating the preconditions. In our example, the goal is "arriving at work on time." The pre-conditions are waking up, dressing, starting the car, and driving to the workplace. The operators for making the conditions work include setting the alarm, replacing a dead car battery, and taking an alternative route if a traffic jam is encountered. Of course, there might be other operators as well, such as filling the gas tank or dropping your daughter off at school.

GPS was designed to solve any problem that could be expressed in this manner. However, the software's design limitations often prevented the program from arriving at the desired goal, with no explanation or alternatives. It was largely because of these limitations that researchers at Stanford University in the mid 1960s developed Dendral, the first pragmatic application of machine reasoning that could be used in the real world. Instead of trying to create a grand algorithm that could solve any problem, the Stanford researchers focused on a single, highly specific problem—the use of mass spectrography to isolate organic compounds.

They developed the AI program by setting out to answer three fundamental questions:

1. What knowledge is needed?
2. How can that knowledge be represented?
3. How can the knowledge be acquired?

As the challenge was of keen interest to chemists, the Dendral project was launched as a collaboration between a group of chemists involved in mass spectrography and computer programmers involved in AI research. The result was a logic-based AI system capable of both backward and forward chaining. If the program failed to satisfy a particular condition, it would leap backward and continue testing other conditions until a successful conclusion was reached. This ability to reiterate as required essentially resolved the fundamental obstacles encountered by GPS.

As the 1960s drew to a close, a number of design teams in the private sector began turning out automated systems based on symbolic processing, for use in industrial training. Drawing from large bases of accepted knowledge and communicating in casual language, these computer-assisted instruction (CAI) programs demonstrated the feasibility of rule-based symbolic prototyping. Importantly, their developers created a large base of investigative knowledge on the nature of learning and the architecture of cognition, knowledge essential to the development of a machine-processable inference system.

In 1971, Automated Medical Laboratories (AML) introduced the first computer-based medical diagnostic system. The

AML project not only contained a broad base of medical expertise, but interfaced directly with diagnostic instrumentation, such as spirometry, electrocardiograph, blood monitoring, and optometry equipment.

The AML system was noteworthy for two reasons. First, it was found that patients were more receptive to divulging intimate details about their bodies and the state of their health to a machine console, than to another human. This principle has since become fundamental to the development of diagnostic systems with computer-patient interfaces. The software (which was written by the author of this book) compiled a comprehensive medical history and was capable of branching to explore specific areas of possible concern based on patient responses. This secondary function has also become an essential design feature in medical diagnostic systems.

Second, the AML lab integrated a diverse suite of diagnostic instruments with a central computer, rather than spewing out a miscellany of printouts that had to be read and then input to one or more computers by a human operator. This process greatly improved the accuracy of diagnostic testing by eliminating human error, and streamlined what would otherwise have been a tedious barrage of procedures.

The most significant advancement toward the practical application of AI programming emerged from the Stanford Heuristic Programming Project (HPP) in 1974. Called MYCIN, the project integrated many of the previously espoused academic theories in such areas as symbolic mathematics, machine heuristics, and knowledge engineering. The project was limited to two tasks: diagnosing bacterial infections and recommending an effective therapeutic regimen.

To use MYCIN, the attending physician sat at a computer terminal connected to a Digital Equipment Corporation mainframe computer. When the program was activated, a dialogue took place between the physician and the expert system. Eventually MYCIN produced a diagnosis and a detailed drug therapy recommendation.

The software took into consideration laboratory results, symptoms manifested by the patient, and general characteristics such as age and sex, before suggesting a diagnosis. After identifying the most likely infectious organisms, MYCIN then prescribed one or more drugs to treat the infection.

To make allowances for uncertainty, the information given to MYCIN could be qualified by a certainty factor expressed as a value between -1 and +1, indicating the physician's degree of confidence in the response to a query. For example, if the physician was only moderately certain that a particular symptom was present, he or she could type "*yes .5*" to indicate a confidence factor of about 50 percent.

If asked to explain its line of investigation, MYCIN would explain what hypotheses it was considering and how the pertinent question would either support or rule out that hypothesis. By way of follow-up, the physician could trace the program's line of reasoning after the diagnosis was made.

At the core of MYCIN was an exhaustive knowledge base, a logic-based processing method, and a symbolic math. In this respect, it was a working model for virtually all AI expert systems in use today and the progenitor of all their designers' cliches.

MYCIN was limited by its reliance on operator input for clinical manifestations and its inability to learn by statistical integration of new results into its database. Despite these limitations, the experiment is widely hailed as a milestone in AI research, and numerous research papers and textbook chapters have been devoted to its design.

The Rise of Expert Machines

Since the 1980s AI research has been almost synonymous with military technology—most prominently, the Defense Advanced Research Project Agency (DARPA) program. In 1985, DARPA research produced a lightweight aluminum robot tank capable of recognizing landscapes, maneuvering independently, and firing without guidance at specified targets. The tank's performance was lackluster in simulated battle conditions, but the mere fact that it could accomplish its missions without human operators was in itself a significant advance in the practical application of AI theory.

In 1982, the Japanese Ministry of International Trade and Industry consummated the fashion in AI research by mandating the Fifth Generation Project. The first four generations of computing were modeled exclusively on von Neumann architecture, the conventional computer design incorporating an arithmetic logic unit and several reusable registers. In contrast, the Japanese team aimed at a fifth generation of computers whose cognitive behavior would be all but indistinguishable from that of humans. The project's focus was distributed among expert systems, natural language programs, voice and vision recognition, robotics, and super-computers. Ultimately, the team failed to achieve its objectives and was disbanded.

Early cognitive computing systems were able to produce judgments with the same—or nearly the same—accuracy as a human expert precisely because their knowledge was derived from human experience. In fact, the effectiveness of these systems were only as strong as the detail of their human-engineered knowledge bases.

The capabilities of rule-based systems were further demonstrated in several mainframe applications, including mineral exploration, computer systems integration, and military intelligence. One of these systems, Prospector, represented a unique convergence of academia, public service, government, and private enterprise. Designed to guide geological exploration for mineral deposits, the program was developed at SRI International under the auspices of the National Science Foundation and the U.S. Geological Survey.

The system performed brilliantly in a test environment but was never implemented on the commercial level. Its design concepts, however, were carried over to a landmark project called Drilling Adviser, a minicomputer-based expert system used to troubleshoot oil drilling problems in the field. For nearly a decade the greater share of this powerful technology has been confined to university and military laboratories.

Today, interest in artificial intelligence is at its peak, fueled by the injection of large capital commitments from the private sector. As a result, recent decades have witnessed a staggering proliferation of products for building cognitive computing systems, culminating in IBM's Watson, popularly known as the all-time champion of champions of the TV quiz show *Jeopardy*.

If you have previously read or heard about Watson, you may have assumed the computer system was named after Sherlock Holmes's sidekick and confidante. If so, you might be surprised to learn the system was named for Thomas J. Watson, the first chairman of the board of International Business Machines. The Watson computer system was actually developed specifically, and some might say, whimsically, to compete on *Jeopardy*. The machine's database included 200 million pages of content, stored not on a hard disk, but in the computer's massive memory chips, enabling nearly instant search and recall of facts. As was widely reported in popular media, the computer system defeated two former "grand champions".

Watson's defining features are its ability to respond to questions posed in natural language, retrieve relevant information from a vast database, mimic human reasoning, and formulate highly probable answers. According to IBM,

> *"more than 100 different techniques are used to analyze natural language, identify sources, find and generate hypotheses, find and score evidence, and merge and rank hypotheses."*

Watson's question-and-answer software is currently being used in commercial environments to analyze legal issues, provide input to investment firms, assist with medical consultations, and generate cooking recipes, among other applications.

The computers developed to date can imitate cognition but not duplicate it. However, current AI research offers the promise of enabling a computer not merely to mimic the heuristic processes that underlie human reasoning, but also to analyze and resolve highly complex problems with a level of efficiency no human can approximate.

In terms of analyzing information, solving problems, and making decisions based on facts, your brain is already obsolete.

AI Milestones

1957	General Problem Solver (GPS) created by Newell, Shaw and Simon
1958	LISP programming language devised by John McCarthy (MIT)
1959	MIT AI Lab founded by John McCarthy and Marvin Minsky
1961	First industrial robot, Unimate, installed on a General Motors assembly line
1968	Dendral, the first rule-based AI system, developed at Stanford to isolate molecular structure of organic compounds
1969	Shakey, the first robot combining locomotion, perception and problem solving, developed at Stanford Research Institute
1969	First International Joint Conference on Artificial Intelligence (IJCAI) held at Stanford
1971	First automated multiphasic medical diagnostic system developed by Automated Medical Laboratories
1972	Prolog programming language developed by Alain Colmerauer
1974	MYCIN medical diagnostic system introduced with physician-computer interface and on-demand feedback
1978	Prospector rule-based system developed for mineral exploration
1982	Fifth Generation Project adopted by Japanese Ministry of International Trade and Industry
1997	Deep Blue defeats world chess champion Garry Kasparov
2000	Nomad robot explores remote regions of Antarctica for meteorite samples

2004	NASA rovers Spirit and Opportunity navigate the surface of Mars autonomously
2004	DARPA Grand Challenge inspires commercial development of self-driving cars
2009	Human Connectome Project launched by the National Institutes of Health to build a circuit diagram of the human brain
2011	IBM Watson defeats Jeopardy game show champions
2015	U.S. Navy launches robotic submarine capable of operating autonomously
2015	SyNAPSE project funded by DARPA launched to replicate one hemisphere of a human brain
2016	Plans to replace human soldiers with robots announced by U.S. Defense Department

5

RAGE, RAGE AGAINST THE DYING OF THE LIGHT

How AI is Changing Your Health

"If you gaze long enough into an abyss, the abyss will gaze back into you."
Friedrich Nietzche

Since its conception, Artificial Intelligence, with its great ambition to understand and duplicate human cognition, has been a truly multidisciplinary endeavor, both contributing to and receiving inspiration from other scientific fields. Especially in medicine, pharmacology, biological research, nanotechnology, and neuroscience, AI may hold the keys to the future quality of life for all humanity.

Artificial Intelligence was first implemented in medical settings to support health care workers with tasks that rely on the manipulation and interpretation of data. For example, an AI medical record system might alert staff when it detects a potential problem with a planned treatment, or significant changes in a patient's condition. AI diagnostic systems linked to large databases of medical information have assisted clinicians and researchers since the 1970s. Because AI systems have the capacity to learn, they hold the potential for the discovery of new phenomena and the creation of new medical knowledge.

In the case of complex or rare medical conditions, AI systems are valuable resources for diagnosis and treatment. AI systems are also used to monitor treatment plans for inconsistencies or errors and omissions, and to formulate treatments for specific conditions based on patient data and accepted treatment guidelines. Many medical images can be interpreted by computers, including X-rays, angiograms, and CT and MRI scans.

DXplain, developed at Massachusetts General Hospital, was designed to assist in diagnosing patient conditions, analyzing clinical findings, such as symptoms and lab results, to produce a ranked list of probable diagnoses. The program offers up a specific justification for each diagnosis, as well as possible avenues for further investigation. In all, DXplain contains a database of over 4,500 clinical manifestations associated with over 2,000 different diseases.

DXplain is in routine use at a number of hospitals and medical schools, for clinical, educational, and consultation uses. As an electronic medical textbook, the system provides a description of over 2,000 different diseases, emphasizing the signs and symptoms that occur in each disease, with recent references for each specific disease.

Clinical Applications

One of the most successful settings in which AI systems are applied is the clinical laboratory. Computer systems are commonly used to interpret test results ordered by practitioners. The PUFF system, first implemented at Presbyterian Medical Center in San Francisco in 1977 was one of the earliest deployments of AI in clinical medicine and, after many thousands of cases, is still in use. GermWatcher checks for hospital-acquired infections, by monitoring microbiology culture data from the hospital's laboratory system.

Machine learning is currently used to develop the knowledge bases used by expert systems. Given a set of clinical cases that act as examples, a machine learning system can produce a systematic description of clinical features that uniquely characterize a specific condition. This knowledge can be expressed in the form of logical "if-then" rules. A classic example of this type of system is the KARDIO program, which was developed to interpret electrocardiogram results.

AI is becoming increasingly vital to patient care, as well. Medical error is the third largest cause of death in the United States. In 2013, at least 250,000 people died not from the illnesses or injuries that prompted them to seek hospital care but from preventable mistakes. That number exceeds deaths from strokes and Alzheimer's combined, and is surpassed only by heart disease and cancer, which each claim about 600,000 lives per year.

Martin Makary, a professor at Johns Hopkins University School of Medicine in Baltimore contends that the death toll from medical mishaps would be even higher if nursing homes and outpatient care were included. "People don't just die from bacteria and heart plaque, but also from communication breakdowns, fragmented healthcare, diagnostic mistakes, and overdosing. Collectively, these events represent the third leading cause of death in the United States...one of the most underreported endemics in global health."

An earlier study estimated the toll at between 250,000 and 440,000 per year. Experts do not know the exact number of people who die from botched surgeries, faulty prescriptions, or a computer glitch simply because no one is keeping count.

One promising solution, the AiCure program uses mobile technology and facial recognition to determine if the right person is taking a given drug at the right time. The data is transmitted to a clinician who confirms if the patient is taking his or her medication as directed. The same technology can also be used to flag adverse events.

One particularly valuable application of machine learning is the discovery of new drugs. Given examples of drugs that exhibit a particular activity, and based upon a description of the chemical structure of those compounds, a learning system can suggest the chemical attributes that are necessary to create that activity, pointing the way for the development of new compounds. Machine learning techniques have been shown to at least equal—and often outperform—analog drug development. An added benefit is the generation of knowledge in a form more easily understood by chemists.

Berg, a private company that applies AI systems to develop diagnostic tools and discover new drugs, formed a partnership with the U.S. Department of Defense, the Parkinson's Institute Clinical Center, and major biotech companies, to accelerate the development of new diagnostic systems and treatments. In 2015, the company teamed with the United Kingdom's National Genomics Project to mine DNA and health data from thousands of British citizens for potential drug targets. The project focuses on patients with rare diseases and six common cancers. According to Niven Narain, Berg's cofounder and president, Berg uses artificial intelligence "to look at patterns in the data to find areas in the biology that are fingerprints of that disease."

Genome Mapping

Nowhere in the research spectrum is Artificial Intelligence more prominent than genome mapping. All the genes in a human body are, in effect, an extremely complicated code. Scientists have been trying to break the code since the early 1900s. Once the code is broken, it will reveal secrets of how the human body works, leading to more effective disease prevention.

In 2000, scientists from the Human Genome Project (HGP) and Celera Genomics announced that they had assembled a working-draft sequence of all the genes in a human body, known collectively as the genome. The accomplishments of the Human Genome Project stand today as one the greatest scientific achievements in history.

A human body has from 26,000 to 40,000 genes, each of which is composed of a unique sequence of pairs. Each such pair has four bases, called base pairs. A single DNA molecule is shaped like a twisted ladder, with its rungs formed by the interlocking bases. Though a human body has about 3 billion base pairs, only about four percent make up DNA that affects gene function. The functions of the other 96 percent "junk DNA," are unknown.

Better understanding the human genome will lead to major advances in preventing or curing diseases. Though the positions of some genes that control the body's medical traits are already known, other genes with as yet unknown functions have also been identified. The point of AI genome research is to determine just what role the mystery genes serve.

In 2016, researchers discovered that, besides the sequencing of pairs, a further, underlying code structure exists in the manner in which DNA molecules are packed together. The meaning of the packing code as yet remains a mystery.

Nanotechnology

Another area of scientific research where AI holds the promise to drive world-changing breakthroughs is nanotechnology.

The term *nano* refers to a length of measurement equal to one-billionth of one meter, approximately the width of ten atoms. Nanotechnology is the branch of engineering devoted to creating nanobots, also known as nanites or nanomachines. A nanobot is a device, only a few atoms in length or width, able to perform a preprogrammed task—in effect, a microscopic robot. Nanobots may be made from almost any type of material, synthetic or biologic. The principal manufacturing method is to stack atoms upon each other in layers to form the desired nanomachine. In a nanomanufacturing publicity stunt, scientists at IBM succeeded in arranging 35 xenon atoms to form a microscopic image of the company's logo.

An inherent drawback to producing nanomachines is their size. Building a device atom by atom is a tedious process, for which no mass production capability exists. Scientists are currently studying the self-replicating properties of DNA as a mechanism for creating nanomachines. Using DNA strands, researchers have created a prototype of a nanobot with two rotating arms capable of responding to chemical reactions.

The most formidable obstacle to the manufacture of nanomachines is the power supply required. One possible solution is nuclear energy—painting a thin layer of radioactive material onto the nanobot's surface. The nanite absorbs energy from the decaying atomic particles, providing the power required to perform its preprogrammed task. Another possibility is human tissue; a biological nanobot could be engineered to ingest body tissue to obtain energy.

Regardless of the design method, a nanobot will ideally perform its task and then dissolve so the body can absorb and excrete it. Silicon, which is durable, flexible, and conducts electricity, will not dissolve in body fluids. Owing to their miniscule size, swarms of nanomachines would be required to perform most tasks. For medical applications, biodegradability will be essential, with so many foreign particles inside the body.

To perform certain tasks, especially in medical applications, controlled mobility is another issue. Nanobots must be capable of migrating to a predetermined site, such as a clog in an artery, and remain in the location to complete their task. Another requirement is that the machine must be able to operate autonomously, independent of outside control. Physical, electrical, and chemical reactions can produce a response, but the introduction of these stimuli rob the device of the advantage of independent operation.

Once these obstacles are overcome, nanobots will be able to repair damaged or diseased tissues at the molecular level. They may be used to attach themselves to specific cells, such as cancer cells, and report the position and structure of these tissues.

Nanotechnology suffers from the physical limitations of its working scale, in which the physics are completely different from that of the macroscopic world. Artificial Intelligence is extremely helpful in surmounting this barrier. "Functional recognition imaging" using artificial neural networks is used to simplify the data and reduce the number of independent variables.

Neural networks have successfully solved the problem of identifying the structural properties of nanomaterials, such as alignment and curvature—a task impossible by ordinary visual inspection.

Real optical images cannot be obtained from nanoscaled devices. Images at this scale must be interpreted from data and translated into digital simulations. Several AI programs currently in use are capable of accurately simulating the interaction of atoms. Such techniques are extremely useful in creating nanoscale images.

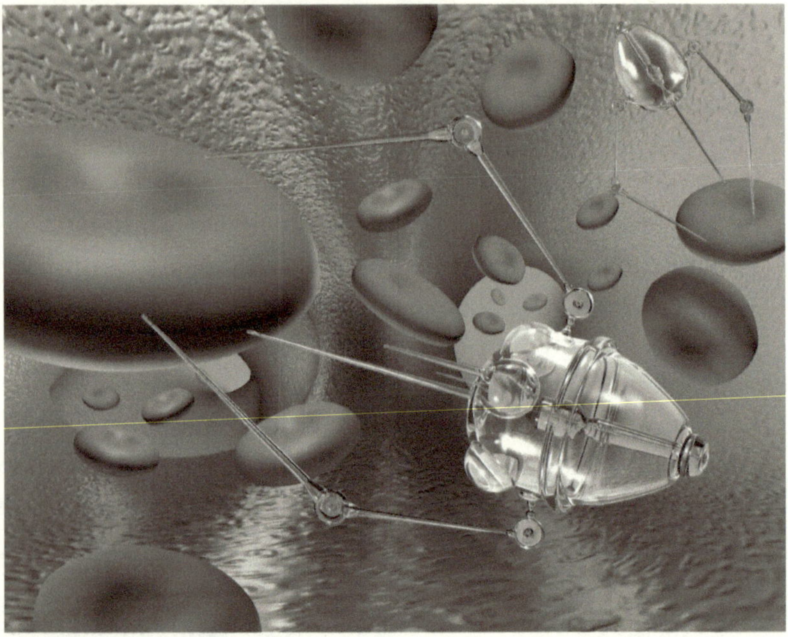

Artist's conception of a nanobot repairing a blood cell.

Medical Robotics

When most people hear the term "artificial intelligence," the image that most often comes to mind is an autonomous, human-like robot. Indeed, robots are being used increasingly in health care, from rehab to the operating room. However, medical robots, at best, are distant relatives from the ambulatory androids of science fiction books and movies.

In popular science, the concept of robots ranges from the toaster-like Robby the Robot in *Forbidden Plant* (who later appeared regularly in the *Lost in Space* television series) to androids in the mold of the *Terminator*. The term robot was first used in a 1921 play, *Rossum's Universal Robots,* by a Czech writer, Karel Capek. According to Capek, the term was suggested by his brother Josef from the Czech word *robota*, meaning servitude. In 1927, Fritz Lang's film Metropolis featured a machine-human (*Maschinenmensch*), played by German actress Brigitte Helm—the first robot depicted in cinema. Isaac Azimov's often cited novel *I, Robot* popularized the notion of mechanical humans in 1942.

The first autonomous robot capable of complex behavior was created by William Grey Walter of the Burden Neurological Institute at Bristol, England in 1948. Walter wanted to prove that connections between a small number of brain cells could give rise to complex behaviors. His tortoise-shaped robots, which he called Elmer and Elsie, were capable of finding their way to a recharging station when they ran low on battery power.

In 1954, George Devol designed a robot that was capable of transferring objects from one point to another within a distance of about twelve feet—the first industrial application of robotics. Devon founded a company called Unimation in 1956 to manufacture the device.

Robotics were first used in medicine for rehabilitation and to assist people with disabilities to perform the activities of daily living or to become integrated into the workplace. In 1963, the so-called "Rancho Arm" was developed to assist handicapped patients at the Rancho Los Amigos Hospital in Downey, California. Five years later, Marvin Minsky created the computer-controlled "Tentacle Arm," with twelve hydraulic joints. In 1988, David Gow constructed a bionic arm, which he called the Edinburgh Modular Arm System (EMAS).

The first robotic system applied in a surgical procedure was the PUMA 560, which was capable of guiding a needle for a brain biopsy under the control of a computer. Later, the Probot system was introduced as an aid to transurethral resection of the prostate. In 1992, IBM developed Robodoc, a robotic system for assisting orthopedic surgeons with total hip replacements.

Currently, medical robotics are able to facilitate operations that are quicker and more accurate than conventional procedures, resulting in shorter hospital stays, greater patient turnover, lower chances of infection, and overall reduction in health care costs. Tiny robot pills are able to reach into areas of the intestinal tract that are difficult to reach by other means. Telerobotics, also known as telepresence technology, allows surgeons to operate at a distance from the operating room.

The original goal of telerobotics research, conducted simultaneously by Stanford Research Institute, the U.S. Department of Defense, and NASA, was to enable surgical robotic arms mounted on an armored vehicle to conduct operations on the battlefield. The result was the widely used robotic surgical system commercially marketed as Da Vinci, incorporating "fingers" three to five millimeters in diameter able to reach much smaller places in the body than a human hand, with less burden to patients.

The benefits of robotics and AI-empowered medical devices are so profound that, in the near future such equipment will become indispensable to the delivery of health care. Surgical robots already in use today can perform intricate procedures, reaching where human hands cannot. Robotics allows for greater accuracy, less invasive surgeries, and less pain to the patient. Devices such as the Da Vinci surgical system allow the surgeon to control the entire surgery while sitting at a console outside the operating room.

The Da Vinci surgical robot creates small incisions of about one to two centimeters, in lieu of much larger cuts required to allow access to a human surgeon's hands. The robot also offers greater visualization of the area where the surgery is performed and superior precision. The seated physician controlling the operation experiences less fatigue and stress, further reducing the random chance of error. Follow-up studies show that the use of surgical robots like the Da Vinci system reduces hospital stays by half, reduces the costs by one third, and results in faster recovery.

The Cyberknife is used for noninvasive cancer treatment. The robot tracks, detects, and attacks tumors by delivering an accurate high dose of chemotherapy directly to cells that have turned cancerous, without damaging surrounding tissues.

Training robots are increasingly replacing cadavers and dummies for use in rehearsing surgical procedures. Robotic mannequins such as the Medsim-Eagle Patient Simulator and the Veterans Affairs Palo Alto System have eyes that open and close, a torso that simulates breathing, and appendages that are capable of movement and swelling.

In a study conducted by surgeons at Children's National Medical Center in Washington, a supervised autonomous robot performed soft-tissue surgery, stitching together a pig's bowel—and doing so better than a human surgeon. According to Peter Kim, associate surgeon in chief at the hospital and project lead on the Smart-Tissue Autonomous Robot, or STAR, "this smart, intelligent technology will tell you how to conduct surgery optimally." Kim contends that surgical robots, rather than replacing human surgeons, will ensure that all patients receive the best care, regardless of which surgeon is available when the need arises.

In the study, the surgical robot's performance was compared to documented results derived from manual surgery. In terms of quality and accuracy, the STAR shined brightly. The machine incorporates a robotic arm with surgical instruments, using imaging technologies and markers to navigate along tissue. The robot makes the decision of where sutures should go, based on vision and pressure, within a range of less than a millimeter.

Whether autonomous robots should be used to perform surgical procedures where human life is at stake raises a number of yet-to-be-addressed liability and ethical concerns.

The majority of medical devices sold in the United States rely on software. A pacemaker typically uses over 80,000 lines of programming, a drug-infusion pump needs 170,000 lines, and an MRI scanner requires more than 7 million lines.

As AI programming and computer hardware become more sophisticated, and knowledge bases continues to expand, medical and scientific exploration will yield benefits only dreamt of in the past. Cures for common cancers, new and more effective drugs, and self-guided disease-treating nano-bots offer the potential to greatly improve the quality of life and extend longevity for future generations.

6

NOT WITH THE EYES BUT WITH THE MIND

How AI is Changing Your Well-Being

"If you can dream it, you can make it so."
Ralph Waldo Emerson

Of all the rapidly advancing technologies focusing on entertainment and well-being, the ones that will have the most immediate impact are Virtual Reality, Brain-Computer Interfaces, and robotics.

Virtual Reality

Mention the term Virtual Reality, and most people will envision someone wearing oversized goggles and gesturing into the air with wired thimbles attached to the fingers. Indeed, even the earliest attempts at creating Virtual Reality games relied primarily on visual stimulation and finger pointing.

In theory, Virtual Reality (VR) refers to any interactive sensory simulation experienced in a three-dimensional environment. In a true VR immersion, the user should be able to behave within the simulation in the same way as in reality—for example, by viewing a virtual room from all angles, or performing surgery on a three-dimensional virtual patient. VR technology is currently used in a diversity of disciplines, including medicine, business, education, and architecture. Inevitably, it will be used for less noble, though possibly even more profitable, applications such as popular entertainment and pornography.

Virtual environments share at least one thing in common with robotics—real-time processing constraints. In order to succeed as a convincing representation of reality, a virtual environment requires smooth, changeable, stop-and-start animation. From a production standpoint, the challenge is Herculean. For one thing, a high frame rate comparable to high definition video is required to sustain the illusion of moving within physical reality. At low frame rates, the illusion degrades into a series of jerking still images.

The algorithm for a virtual environment is expressed as a "scene graph," a hierarchical structure representing all the components linked together. The more complex the graph, the more difficult it becomes to maintain a high frame rate. Regardless of the frame rate, the LOD (Level of Detail) is critical to a convincing illusion. For example, portrayed objects need to become more detailed as the Virtual Reality user "approaches" them.

VR isn't just about computer games and entertainment. Since the late 1990s, VR technology has been explored for medical applications including training, diagnosis, and treatment. The Virtual Visual Environment Display (VIVED) was developed by NASA Johnson Space Center in conjunction with LinCom Corporation, the University of Texas at Galveston, and the Galveston Independent School District. VIVED provides a unique educational experience using VR technologies, integrating "fly-throughs" of the human skull and heart with interactive audio and video.

Tiny slices of a human skull and MRI slices of a heart were used to create images for the virtual environment. Scans of the skull were performed resulting in a data set of over 120 slices through the skull and 60 slices through the mandible (jaw).

An MRI scan of the human heart resulted in a data set containing 200 slices. A Silicon Graphics Reality Engine computer was used to turn the slices into three-dimensional images and movies in which the participant "flies through" the body. The result was a self-contained educational experience allowing students to interactively tour a human heart or skull.

Potential applications for this technology include any area requiring an understanding of complex three-dimensional relationships, such as anatomy, mechanical engineering, chemistry, pathology, plastic and reconstructive surgery, and endoscopy. Surgical simulations may become routine, especially to rehearse strategies for intricate and rare operations.

In architecture and engineering, VR technology currently enables contractors, developers, and end users to visualize the end product of their project before it's even under construction. The benefits include the ability to eliminate mock-ups, facilitating decisions early in the planning process, and proceeding to construction with a better understanding of the end product. The Vizard-powered Architecture Interactive (AI) software platform allows architects, engineers, and contractors to streamline design reviews by creating interactive and immersive VR simulations.

VR devices are now commonly used by many car and aeronautics companies, to test product designs and simulate user interaction. Head-mounted VR displays are also used in flight simulators.

The wearable Sensics XSight VR device, which makes use of six displays to present an enlarged compound image to each eye, is mainly used by academics and engineers, as well as in military training.

Motion Analysis's motion-tracking technology is based on a suit covered with markers that emit light to near-infrared cameras arranged around the wearer. The cameras create a digital skeletal model that the system can then map to a virtual image. A 3D head-mounted display enables the wearer to "see" his or her virtual hands move in real-time in the virtual environment, within an accuracy of about one millimeter. The system is specifically aimed at engineers interested in exploring virtual models of their design concepts.

An electronic glove devised by CyberGlove captures and translates a user's finger movements with high precision, empowering wearers to interact with virtual objects in real-time in a natural way. The glove is currently used for training, defense, and engineering.

People familiar with or interested in Virtual Realty often think of the Oculus Rift headset, which can be controlled by an electronic glove. Potential applications for the Rift range from 3D computer games to scientific uses such as surgery rehearsal and archaeology simulation. Similarly, Microsoft has heavily promoted its wearable Hololens device, which augments rather than simulates reality, projecting images into the user's eyes.

A comparable augmented reality device, the Daqri smart helmet, uses an Intel RealSense 3D camera to overlay images on the wearer's natural view. For example, an electrician might use the device to see real-time wiring schematics. A 360-degree array of sensors tracks the wearer's movement and vision and provides instructions on how to carry out a task. Wearers can effectively peer into the internal workings of any real object for which augmented reality programming has been developed.

The devices that enable VR users to "touch" and "feel" simulated objects in a virtual environment are referred to as *haptic* interfaces. The term is derived from the Greek word *haptikos* meaning "touchable." In a realistic VR immersion, the user should be able to touch a virtual object and experience a response. This type of interaction is referred to as haptic feedback.

Two types of haptic feedback are important in a VR simulation: tactile and force. Tactile feedback refers to the sensation produced by touching an object. Examples include texture, temperature, and vibration. Force feedback includes weight, resistance, and inertia.

Using a haptic interface, a VR user is able to touch, feel and manipulate three-dimensional objects within a VR immersion. A true haptic interface is a two-way device; i.e., the user's physical actions create input, which in turn results in a simulated event, such as a door or window being opened.

Haptic devices are relatively sophisticated in comparison to other digital interfaces, such as pointing devices and joysticks. Responding to sensations requires a much faster refresh rate than visual feedback.

Haptic interfaces are classified as ground-based or body-based. Ground-based devices include force-reflecting joysticks and linkage-based constructs such as robot arms. Body-based devices, more commonly used in VR systems, include interactive gloves and suits.

Brain-Computer Interfaces

Conventional VR technology relies on visual stimulation and interactive pointing. However, interest in direct electrical stimulation of the brain has been explored since the 1970s. The idea of a VR helmet with electrodes attached to various receptors in the brain has long titillated scientists and enthusiasts with the premise of producing artificially induced experiences that are literally indistinguishable from reality. Such research has actually led to advances in the "deep brain" treatment of a variety of diseases.

Bioelectric medicine uses electrical stimulation to switch off chronic pain, as well as diagnose, monitor, and control inflammatory disease. Deep-brain stimulation has already been applied to patients with Parkinson's disease and holds the promise of treating such diseases as rheumatoid arthritis, lupus, diabetes, hepatitis, hypertension, bowel disease, and other chronic conditions.

The central focus of most of this research is the vagus nerve, which sends signals from the brain to the gastro-intestinal tract, heart, liver, spleen, and other organs. Infection or injury creates a biochemical imbalance, the changes are relayed to motor neurons in the brain, which send back signals to the affected organ to regulate the chemicals that produce inflammatory reactions throughout the body. Bioelectric stimulation aims to control this immune response by shocking the circuits that control the immune system and thereby harness them to treat inflammatory diseases. Results so far suggest that this approach will help treat disorders such as rheumatoid arthritis, multiple sclerosis, and possibly even diabetes and cancer.

The development of new techniques to identify and control the nervous system's pathways responsible for inflammatory responses is proceeding rapidly. In 2011, a vagus nerve stimulator was implanted just beneath the collarbone of a patient suffering from crippling rheumatoid arthritis. Within weeks, he was nearly pain free and, four years after the surgery, remaining in total remission without steroids.

In 2015, the U.S. Food and Drug Administration approved the use of a vagus nerve stimulator to treat obesity. The National Institutes of Health (NIH) funded the $250 million project Stimulating Peripheral Activity to Relieve Conditions (SPARC), and DARPA has launched Electrical Prescriptions (ElectRx) to advance bioelectric technology research. Inevitably, bioelectric medicine will replace or augment the drugs currently prescribed for the treatment of inflammatory diseases.

Bioelectric treatment has also been implemented successfully to treat severe depression. PET (Positron Emission Tomography) scans were used to map areas of the brain that exhibited marked changes during periods of depression, revealing increased blood flow in certain regions of the middle brain. Conversely, areas of the brain responsible for positive motivation exhibited decreased activity. The specific location of the brain responsible for depression was pinpointed in a small area called the *subcallosal cingulate* area, which functions as a hub for decision making, emotional responses, and memory retention.

This finding led to a revolutionary treatment, by surgically implanting electrodes close to the *subcallosal cingulate* to send an electrical current through the associated neural circuits.

Deep brain stimulation has been used since 2002 to treat Parkinson's Disease. The effectiveness of the technology has generated interest among researchers to apply the technique for other maladies such as bipolar disorder, obsessive-compulsive disorder, and Tourette's syndrome.

In 1954, in a now-famous research project probing the origins of pleasure, psychologists James Old and Peter Milner at McGill University attached electrodes deep inside the brains of rats and then observed the rats' responses to tiny jolts of electric current administered to various regions of their brains. The rats were able to control the stimulation by pressing levers. When the current was directed to certain areas of the brain called the *septum* and the *nucleus accumbens*, the rats obsessively activated the lever, up to 2,000 times per hour. Given a choice of eating or pressing the lever, the rats preferred the lever every time—even to the point of starvation. The researchers' conclusion was that they had discovered the "pleasure center" in the rats' brains.

In an ethically debatable follow-up study with human subjects, while attempting to devise a "cure" for homosexuality, Robert Heath at Tulane University reproduced similar behavior in response to deep brain stimulation. The subject, referred to by the code name B-19, was given the opportunity to activate the pleasure center in his own brain at will. Subsequently, he obsessively pressed the lever 1,500 times in an hour. However, it became clear from B-19's own testimony that the stimulation had not caused intense pleasure at all, but only "wanting"—unrelenting motivation to continue receiving the stimulation.

More recent research has established that the brain mechanisms responsible for experiencing pleasure, especially from food and sex, overlap with higher-order pleasures such as monetary, artistic, and altruistic gratification. All sensations of pleasure, whether sensory or aesthetic, involve the same fundamental regions of the brain. Scientists have identified three separate brain-related components of pleasure: wanting, liking, and learning. A person can "want" a reward without necessarily "liking" it, as occurs in addiction.

The processes by which the brain creates pleasure are called hedonic mechanisms. The specific locations where these processes originate are found deep in the brain, but also in the overlying layer, the cortex. The hedonic hotspots are each no more than a cubic millimeter in a rat's brain, and a cubic centimeter in a human brain.

Fundamentally, pleasure evolved as a reward for fulfilling the imperatives of survival and procreation. Consequently, the most immediate and profound rewards are derived from food and sex. Scientists at Oxford University mapped a portion of the orbitofrontal cortex of the brain, a small center behind the eyes, associated with pleasure related to food and sex.

The advancement of brain mapping and deep brain stimulation will inexorably lead to the creation of Virtual Reality environments by surgical implantation of electrodes in the brain. Such environments, rather than relying on projected images and electronic gloves, will be portrayed and played in the mind, enabling the human subject to actually experience recorded scenarios as if they are taking place in real life.

Such Brain-Computer Interfaces (BCIs) have already been used to enable a human to operate a robot hand by means of thought control, and to resurrect memories in laboratory mice of how to perform certain repetitive actions.

An intriguing and potentially revolutionary development in BCI technology is a telepathic "brain gate" capable of linking the brains of separate individuals. In 2013, researchers created an electronic link between the brains of two rats separated by thousands of miles. The technology to link human brains in the same way currently exists. However, much must be learned about how well a human brain can adapt to such a link, how many implants would be required, and where they would need to be positioned.

The first obstacle is increasing the bandwidth required to transmit meaningful information between the brains. The most sophisticated systems currently in use have only about 100 electrodes, whereas a human brain has more than 100 billion neurons. In other words, millions of electrodes will be required to enable even the simplest inter-brain communication. The major challenge isn't the electronics, which are easily built, but the architecture—arranging the circuits so that the brain receives and comprehends both incoming and outgoing signals. Beyond sending and receiving speech, such information as the sharing of experiences, memories, or knowledge are uncharted territory.

The current electronic devices used for brain gate experiments are EEG sensors, which, unfortunately, have poor resolution. Each sensor receives signals from millions of neurons, as well as electrical noise from muscles and the environment. Internal brain electrodes are capable of receiving more data from smaller regions, but require brain surgery. Bandwidth is a gargantuan problem. The bandwidth requirements of a human brain are in the area of tens of terabits per second, far beyond the fastest wireless internet connection. (A terabit is 1,000 trillion bits.) However, researchers theorize that at a maximum neural firing rate of only 25 gigabits, two brains could be connected via implanted multi-electrode arrays such that both resemble one mind.

Realistically, neural interfacing between humans is not likely to occur in the near future; safety, convenience, and a clearly defined need will be required before the considerable financial and research resources would even become available. Using current technology, a telepathic network could be developed within a few years; however, the fidelity would be considerably worse than tin cans connected by a taut string. Language-based communication—i.e., telepathic "speech"—may not even be possible.

When and if brain gate technology is perfected, the issue of privacy will loom large. Merging your own mind with someone else's will expose to each other your thoughts, knowledge, and ideas, but also your innermost fantasies, hidden prejudices, and secret memories. "Remember that time when you were twelve years old and...?" Like it or not, your brain mate will remember it, too.

Love and Sex with Robots

Arguably no visual technology has ever been as perfectly suited to the pornography industry as Virtual Reality. Pornography has existed since the first Homo Sapiens began carving images on cave walls, rocks, and, later, urns. Just as videotapes, DVDs, and internet streaming brought sexually explicit content from theaters into homes, Virtual Reality will eventually eclipse even those developments.

As with any form of pornography, erotic virtual environments dehumanize the actors. Nevertheless, erotic media have always been based on fantasizing—about exotic experiences beyond accepted norms, abandoning inhibitions, desiring and being desired. Catering to the fantasy, a pornographic genre called POV (Point of View) emerged, in which the photographer creates the illusion that the viewer is a participant rather than a voyeur. VR pornography is the ultimate POV expression, in which the observer inhabits the virtual scene.

The essence of the VR experience is the illusion of presence, created by the brain tricking the body into reacting with the visual stimuli as if in reality. For example, if you are immersed in a scene teetering on the edge of the Grand Canyon, you experience vertigo. If you find yourself on a riverboat that begins to move downstream, you experience motion. Whether sexual content in a virtual environment can induce the same sort of brain trick will determine (along with ethical, legal, and social concerns) the future success or demise of VR pornography.

Nevertheless, pornography is a $97 billion industry, consisting less of organized crime syndicates than tens of thousands of entrepreneurs and independently run "studios." VR pornography will inexorably transform the entire adult entertainment industry, obsoleting virtually every film, print magazine, website, erotic toy, and blow-up sex doll found in an adult boutique today. However, since even the lowest priced VR equipment is still expensive by middle class standards, the transformation will undoubtedly remain an elitist privilege, on a par with luxury automobiles and Rolex watches, for years to come.

In principle, sexbots—robots intended to mimic the appearance and traits of a human sexual companion—are a tactile form of Virtual Reality pornography. A sexbot is in effect a simulation, designed to be manipulated by its user and providing both tactile and force feedback. Of course, a blow-up sex doll has the same conceptual qualities. It might be argued that sexbots, no matter how "interactive," are little different from blow-up dolls in terms of psychic benefits. If Virtual Reality pornography and sexbots represent the future of sexual relationships, a thoughtful discussion about the ethics of gender stereotypes and sexual expression looms large on the horizon.

In 2007, a British chessmaster, David Levy, published *Love and Sex with Robots*, a book that reviewers found "troublingly arousing." According to Levy, "love with robots will be as normal as love with other humans." He predicted "a huge demand from people who have a void in their lives because they have no one to love, and no one who loves them. The world will be a much happier place because all those people who are now miserable will suddenly have someone."

Cultural analyst Sherry Turkle believes that people may eventually prefer the kinship of machines to relationships with real people and animals. Not everyone in the scientific community believes this would be a good thing. Kathleen Richardson, a senior research fellow in the ethics of robotics at De Montfort University and director of the Campaign Against Sex Robots believes that "David Levy is taking people's insecurities and offering a solution that doesn't exist."

The prototype sexbot, called Roxxxy, is an automated mannequin with a selection of preprogrammed personalities, including "Wild Wendy," "Mature Martha," "Young Yoko," and "Frigid Farrah." Wild Wendy is experimental and malleable, whereas Young Yoko is inexperienced and anxious to learn. Mature Martha has a wealth of sexual skills, but Frigid Farrah requires coaxing. The sexbot has the same sexual appetites as her owner, but also experiences mood changes and even gets sleepy.

However refined they may become, robots will always be distinguishable from humans. This distinction is referred to as the "uncanny valley"—a point at which a robot's similarity to a human creates uneasiness or revulsion.

The sociological issues of VR pornography and sexbots are similar. Are they harmful activities? Do they augment or detract from reality? Do they dehumanize? Each person has his or her own answers to these questions, based on acquired moral, ethical, and intellectual values.

The immense size of the industry alone bears witness to society's variable moral acceptance for pornography in general. It is reasonable to assume that VR as a pornographic medium will not only permeate society but create new forms of controversy. Manufacturers of VR equipment have declared that they will not prevent or prohibit pornographic content.

Ethicists already argue about whether such media should be classified as prostitution, or if a married person having sexual relationships with a VR performer or a sexbot should constitute adultery.

Nevertheless, reasoning and moral instincts are not the sum of human existence, which, for better or worse, is profoundly influenced by biological influences—not the least of which, the inherited urge to engage in reproductive behavior. Fundamentally, any sexual act involving an object or device is simply masturbation.

That's Entertainment

Any discussion of entertainment robots would be incomplete without mentioning the contributions of Disney Enterprises. The entertainment conglomerate has been designing entertainment robots since the 1950s for use in its theme parks. From dancing bears to singing pirates, Disney's "imagineers" have created thousands of robots.

Some entertainment robots are little more than rolling, remote-controlled speaker phones with video camera "eyes." Such devices, such as those manufactured by Florida Robotics, are routinely marketed for corporate promotions and private parties. The company also makes more complex robots that have the capability to talk with onlookers and include fiber optic hair, remote controlled water guns, an onboard video camera and transmitter, and sound effects. Disney makes use of a Florida Robotics robot called "X1846" at Walt Disney World in Orlando, Florida, to serve drinks to customers.

Entertainment as an industry is larger than science and technology, oil, health care, real estate, fashion, or automobiles. Immense fortunes are made by people seeking to entertain us and those who propel, promote, and propagate them. More money will be spent on AI entertainment in the coming years than on all scientific research projects combined. In this respect, human values have changed little since ancient times, when sexual orgies were commonplace and vast throngs packed the arenas where gladiators fought to the death for the sake of entertainment.

It can be argued that our values—or more precisely, our innate instincts inherited through evolution—have not changed much since the dawn of humankind, and that virtual reality and sexbots are merely logical extensions of those instincts. The pursuit of well-being is deeply ingrained in each of us.

No machine, no matter how sophisticated, will ever know what that's like.

If sex with robots represents the future of sexual relationships, a thoughtful discussion about gender stereotypes looms large on the horizon.

7

TOOTHPASTE, CARS, AND YOUR ROMANTIC PROSPECTS

How AI is Changing Business and Work

"Intelligence is the art of good guesswork."
H. B. Barlow

AI is often envisioned as the rise of self-aware humanoid robots, but in fact, machine intelligence is more commonly applied to a broad range of relatively mundane tasks. Few of us yet interact with robots or ride in self-controlled drones, but our daily lives are increasingly affected by AI systems that can recognize speech or images, make crucial decisions, or analyze patterns of our online behavior.

Since the 1960s, AI has been used to mine for profits, streamline business environments, and cultivate customer buying behavior. As of this writing, AI is present in almost all forms of enterprise, from banks, health care providers, and insurance companies to manufacturers, utility companies, and website marketers. In the corporate workplace, AI is widely used for complex problem solving and decision support in disciplines ranging from financial management to forecasting.

It is a characteristic of modern economies that data increases exponentially literally day by day. Analyzing this growing body of information and formulating quick and accurate decisions requires complex cognitive abilities available only to machine intelligence.

If you live in North America, Europe, or Australia, from the moment the alarm clock wakens you each morning to the moment you turn out the light on the nightstand each night, AI already affects you more than any scientific or cultural phenomenon has influenced people at any previous time in history (with the possible exception of nuclear weapons). As the future unfolds, the impact of AI on your personal life, work, leisure time, and health will continue to multiply.

However, there will be no "Ah ha!" moment, when you suddenly realize that machine intelligence has become indispensable to your existence. It will simply happen, and, if you're like most people, you'll accept it as a normal—and perhaps necessary—event in your everyday life.

Today, the toothpaste you use, the clothing you put on, the vehicle you drive to work, the tools of your trade, the grocery items you purchase, your entertainment choices, and—if you happen to be single—even your romantic outlook, are likely designed, engineered, produced, marketed, inventoried, or referred to you as a result of AI technology. In the rapidly encoraching future, you may not even have to drive your own vehicle. In fact, you might not even have to show up for work, if yours is one of the 9.1 million jobs that will be replaced by intelligent machines by the year 2025 in the United States alone.

Technology advancements have historically obsoleted workers in some fields, and the trend inexorably will increase with the introduction of more machines that are more intelligent. New entrants into the work force will require training to program, maintain, and work with intelligent machines. Nevertheless, the odds of technology-related job loss concentrated at the lower end of the income scale are high. As the AI boom continues, there is every likelihood that not only rank-and-file employees but also executives at all levels of management will be affected by the proliferation of intelligent machines.

One reason for the AI boom is the analytical power made possible by artificial neural networks (ANNs) using fuzzy logic (as described in Chapter 3). In some applications, such as fraud detection, AI has already become the technology of preference. In addition, the use of neural networks has become an established methodology for pattern recognition, particularly of images, data streams and complex data sources. Such networks have emerged as the platform for the majority of data-mining tools currently in use.

Besides fraud detection, machine intelligence is used to analyze and manage consumer buying habits and coordinate production and delivery schedules based on fluctuating customer demand. By eliminating downtime due to unpredictable scheduling changes, AI systems increase productivity.

The Ascent of AI in Business

The basis for all free-market enterprise consists of three interconnected influences: cost, competition, and demand. Commerce originated in ancient times on the basis of products that fulfilled identifiable needs, such as tools, food, or apparel. Today, even products that seem to fulfill only psychic or imaginary needs have a basis in human behavior that can be quantified. For example, "moon rocks," which arguably serve no practical purpose, fulfill a psychic need to experience the pleasure of possessing—or, perhaps, merely the act of purchasing—such a product.

Pricing is as important as a product that fulfills identifiable needs. From the user's standpoint, pricing determines not only how much a product costs, but also its value—the quality in relation to the price. From a marketer's perspective, pricing determines how much money will be made from sales and, in the final analysis, whether or not the business will be successful. In every transaction, users also pay other costs besides the monetary price; real product costs fall into the following categories:

1. Monetary costs
2. Location costs
3. Temporal costs
4. Sensory costs
5. Psychic costs

The monetary cost is based not only upon the purchase price but also upon additional charges such as taxes and freight. However, customers also have to pay location costs such as shipping or transportation. The time spent traveling and shopping represent another type of cost. In addition, some buyers may experience a sensory cost in adjusting to unfamiliar surroundings, and a psychic cost in the form of stress, discomfort, or fear.

A robust forecasting program takes all these types of costs into account. Automated pricing strategies are based on predefined planning processes used to set the final monetary price to the purchaser. Traditional pricing strategies may be as simple as adding a fixed percentage or amount to the cost, or as complicated as a yield management policy.

The seller pays a cost for every product that is sold to a user. To produce a profit, the price received from the user must be higher than the cost paid by the seller. For a business to be profitable, the total revenues received from sales must exceed the total manufacturing costs plus the operating costs of the company. Thus, prices must be high enough to compensate for products that are not sold. Yet, if prices are too high, customers will be discouraged from buying. If prices are too low, the business sacrifices profits that it might otherwise have realized.

Forecasting—the analytics devoted to estimating future events—is fundamental to all aspects of management. The goals of forecasting are to reduce uncertainty and to provide benchmarks for monitoring actual performance. AI forecasting methods are used to predict product demand, inventory levels, worker requirements, surplus rates, and raw materials.

The classic business forecasting dilemma is a scenario known as the Baker's Dozen. Assume a baker bakes 12 loaves of bread and, by the end of that day, eight loaves are sold, leaving a surplus rate of 25 percent (four loaves). The following day, the baker bakes eight loaves, and at closing time all the loaves have been sold. However, the possibility exists that if more loaves had been baked, some of the extra loaves might have been sold as well.

The problem, from a forecasting perspective, is to determine the optimal number of loaves required to maximize sales while minimizing surplus, as cost, competition, and demand fluctuate. Deep learning systems are able optimize inventory while responding to external factors such as changes in economic conditions and supply constrictions.

With the rise of online purchasing and social media, AI began to be applied to collecting, processing, and analyzing information on a massive scale, giving rise to the pop-science terms Big Data, deep learning, and data mining.

Mining for Your Data

Big Data, in a general sense, refers to a very large and rapidly growing volume of information beyond the ability of conventional computer technology to process efficiently. In a typical enterprise environment, the information results from internet usage, social media, and computing task such as word processing or accounting. However, if you ask ten professionals in computer-related fields to define Big Data, the chances are that you will receive at least seven different definitions.

To an online retailer, Big Data is composed of all the information collected from every user, especially buyers, as well as the results of analyzing that information. To a physicist, Big Data consists of all the information generated by humans, the media, and computers. Virtually every entity that has a reason to use the buzzword in its literature and media has its own "take" slanted toward its own interests. Regardless of the slant, analytics and data mining are integral to harnessing and harvesting it.

In logic, analytics refers to the logical science of analysis. In data mining, analytics involves the entire process of collecting, analyzing, and drawing conclusions from a growing body of data. From a business perspective, analytics enables management to view, at any point in time, how customers or users utilize a product or service, as well as demographic and behavioral traits, such as age, gender, buying habits, personal interests, and so forth.

Data mining gives companies a precise view of how particular segments of the customer base react to a product or service, and proposes changes consistent with those findings. In addition to exploring customers' buying patterns, analytics enables management to react much more quickly to marketplace changes. The results enable management to refresh marketing models on the fly, based on each new incoming piece of customer information, to create a more targeted offering.

Data mining techniques are largely identical to those used by computer viruses. In fact, programs that infect computers with programs designed to provide feedback about the internet browsing habits of users are classified as malware in most antivirus databases, as are programs designed to deliver targeted advertisements.

Like a virus, a data mining program secretly intrudes on a user's computer without permission. The program seeks out specific locations on the computer, such as email folders and places where downloads and preferences are stored, and then harvests pertinent data about the user. The program's instructions are in the form of "scripts" that waken automatically when a user accesses the web page to which they are attached.

Data mining scripts are now present on most e-commerce web pages, as well as the sites of many governments and institutions. The information they extract from users' computers is used to create custom product offerings, compile demographic data, and guard against fraud, but also to generate email lists for target marketing ("spam").

Most merchandising websites track customer purchases so that the most relevant products can be displayed each time the user accesses the site. Consumers' buying habits are often sold to other marketers for use in email campaigns or pop-up ads.

Merely reaping information and storing it in a big database are, by themselves, of minimal use. To be meaningful—and, of utmost importance to businesses, also profitable—the mined data must be sorted into identifiable patterns and relationships, or behaviors. Once these behaviors are defined, they then need to be validated. The Data Mining process thus occurs in three separate stages: exploration, pattern definition, and validation.

From a marketing perspective, the resulting information can be used to predict future behaviors, such as purchasing similar or related products. The data can also reveal personal traits, such as age, gender, occupation, hobbies, entertainment preferences, and health status. For example, analytics would predict that a computer user who browses for women's hair coloring and anti-wrinkle cream is most likely a female 40 years or older. Based on statistics about 40-year-old females, the program might predict that the user would also be interested in a certain style of apparel.

Left to its own devices, a data mining system may develop subtle patterns that might otherwise evade normal expectations. A classic case is a supermarket that prominently juxtaposed displays of beer and diapers, creating a seemingly humorous correlation between alcohol consumption and urinary urgency. The displays were actually based on predictive modeling derived from data mining, showing that fathers who have infants and shop on Saturday tend to buy beer and diapers. The model was validated by a surge in sales of both items.

The focus of Data Mining systems is centered on defining behaviors that are useful in generating reliable predictions. Web tracking—identifying and correlating websites visited by a single user—has become a common instrument for mining data about internet users. In an experiment performed by researchers at Princeton University, Google Analytics web tracking scripts were found on more than 70% of the websites they studied. DoubleClick, an especially popular ad-serving system, also developed by Google, was found on half of the sites. The researchers used software that was developed at Princeton, called OpenWPM, to robotically survey one million sites, logging any tracking technology that was detected.

When embedded on a large number of sites, web tracking scripts can compile detailed profiles of individual users navigating the internet. Among the documents leaked by Edward Snowden was a memo indicating that the U.S. National Security Agency tapped into Google's web tracking system to identify potential suspects for surveillance.

In theory, data mining techniques are based on predictive analysis using behavioral modeling and statistics. However, methods such as Google's ad-serving technique actually have built-in biases. Advertisers choose the types of users to target. To streamline the validation process, businesses often rely on heuristic shortcuts; for example, a male who browses female swimsuit photos might be presented, without any statistical basis, with an ad for an erectile dysfunction medication.

Predictably, the practice of data mining has led to controversy over privacy and ethical concerns.

AI in Human Resources

In the workplace, AI has found a natural fit in human resources, training and development, and work automation. The extent and speed of the adoption of AI technologies may determine the cultural and social risks.

In the context of Human Resource (HR) management, AI is used increasingly to source, recruit, manage, and develop employees. A robust HR system captures the behavioral attributes of candidates and compares them to the technical and social requirements of the job. Machine learning techniques enable the department to track successful candidates as they move through the organization, identifying personality traits and skills that relate to potential advancement.

Neural networks and fuzzy logic theory are promising candidates for human resource information systems (HRIS). Analytics is used to form judgments about the appointment of managers, evaluate performance, and provide decision support for personnel decisions.

Developments in computer image recognition are already transforming the workplace. Using fuzzy logic, computers can recognize objects, such as furniture and products, as well as animals, and within a few years will be able to distinguish and identify individuals. Security systems will benefit from the ability of video surveillance to distinguish people with authorized access to a building or office, from those without authorization.

With computer vision and improved language processing ability, machines will be able to identify items and better know how to interact with them. Self-driving vehicles are an example. Image recognition in health care environments will enable machines to interpret and analyze X-ray and MRI images. Humanoid robots with deep learning capability are already being deployed as virtual office receptionists, assembly line workers, and companions for the elderly or debilitated.

Though applications of AI in business may seem rudimentary today, the rise of anthropomorphic robots in the workplace is on the way—assuming the economy of the future is capable of sustaining the not inconsiderable resources required to develop, build, program, and adopt humanoid robot technology. People and robots already work side by side in some workplaces, including manufacturing, health care, and research environments. In most cases, robots working on factory lines are kept in cages, because they pose too many physical risks to humans. As a result, human workflow is kept separate from robot workflow.

Industrial robots are true marvels of engineering and an indispensable part of today's large manufacturing processes. Intelligent robots have taken over many of the tasks in factory operations requiring high degrees of precision, speed, and endurance. In recent years, industrial robots have become increasingly smarter, more flexible, and more autonomous, with the capacity to make decisions and work independently of humans.

The first mobile robot capable of reasoning about its surroundings, called Shakey, was built in 1970 by the Stanford Research Institute. The device featured multiple sensory inputs, including video cameras, laser range finders, and "bump sensors"—micro switches that detect when the robot has collided with an external object—to facilitate navigation.

From 1980, industrial robots began to be made in large numbers, with built-in microprocessors, artificial intelligence, and a higher degree of operational freedom.

As robots become smarter due to neural networks and fuzzy logic, it will become essential that robots and humans adapt to become productive teammates. Toward that end, researchers at Massachusetts Institute of Technology are striving to reverse-engineer the human brain to enable robots to behave more like people.

A smart robot would have the following traits:

1. It can learn from its environment.
2. It can work alongside a human and learn from that interaction.
3. It can learn from its own experiences and improve its work performance accordingly.

Two notable examples are the Baxter and Sawyer collaborative robots built by Rethink Robotics, based in Boston, Massachusetts. Humanoid in appearance, the robots are capable of working side by side with human factory workers, performing highly repetitive tasks such as precision packing, circuit board testing, and assembly line tending. Sensors enable Baxter and Sawyer to adapt to their environment—for example, by gauging the speed of a conveyer belt.

The opinions of experts are currently divided regarding the effect that widespread AI adoption will have on the job market and workplace culture. According to a study by the World Economic Forum (WEF), by 2020 about seven million jobs will be lost—but only two million gained—as a result of technological change in fifteen major developed and emerging economies. Women, according to the report, will be the biggest victims. While men will see approximately one job gained for every three lost, women face more than five jobs lost for every one gained.

It is certain that AI will continue to develop rapidly, with a potential for significant economic and social upheaval.

Occupations Most at Risk from Automation

Job Title	%
Loan officers	98
Receptionists and clerks	96
Legal assistants	94
Retail sales	92
Taxi drivers/chauffeurs	89
Security guards	84
Bartenders	77
Financial advisers	58
Newspaper reporters	11
Musicians	7
Attorneys	3

(Source: Oxford University)

8

THE DATA WILL CONFESS TO ANYTHING

How AI is Changing Your Personal Wealth

"If you cannot accurately predict the future then you must flexibly be prepared to deal with various possible futures."
Edward de Bono

Free-market economies have changed little since the time of the Roman Empire, when the debts of enterprises, as well as individuals, were traded freely for profit. The New York Stock Exchange was founded by Alexander Hamilton, the first U.S. Treasurer, for the purpose of trading government debts. Eventually, stocks of companies were included in the exchange.

Originally, stocks represented an ownership share in the company that issued them. Over time, stock prices were deemed by investors to represent the overall worth of the issuing entity, taking into account its assets, cash flow, and financial position. Early trading strategies were based on the analysis of the potential value of a company's stock in relation to its offering price. Since the 1990s, actual worth has declined in importance in relation to human sentiment, expressed as the reaction to current events, personal opinions, and intuition about the future. Driven by price manipulation, with little or no relation to the actual worth of the issuing company, today's stock markets are often compared to casino gambling and lotteries.

Stock Valuation Methods

One of the oldest methods of valuating stocks is Technical Analysis, based on a process developed by a Japanese rice trader named Homma Munehisa in the 18th century. Munehisa meticulously recorded rice sales day by day for several years, enabling him to track prices and identify upward and downward trends. He observed that prices were heavily influenced by the emotions of traders. So successful was Munehisa that he served as a personal financial adviser to the Japanese emperor and was awarded the title of honorary Samurai, after accumulating one of the most prodigious fortunes in recorded history.

Modern Technical Analysis owes many of its principles to a series of Wall Street Journal editorials authored by Charles H. Dow from 1900 until his death in 1902. The editorials reflected Dow's observations on how the stock market behaved and its overall reflection of the health of the economy. Dow believed that the stock market as a whole was a reliable measure of business conditions and that, by analyzing the overall market, it is possible to identify major market trends, as well as the likely direction of individual stocks. Dow gave substance to his theory by creating the Dow Jones Industrial Index and the Dow Jones Transportation Index (originally called the Rail Index).

Dow Theory involves the study of historical factors that influence a specific stock price over time, from price trends to the emotional response of investors to current events. A so-called bull market, in which stock prices are rising, begins with a primary upward trend referred to as the accumulation phase. A second stage, the public participation phase, occurs as optimism builds, encouraged by improved business conditions and economic data. The last stage in the upward trend is the excess phase, when major investors begin selling off their holdings to those entering the market and unaware that the trend is about to peak. Bull markets are followed by bear markets, an all-consuming downward trend ultimately resulting in massive sell-offs motivated by panic.

Technical Analysis is based on four assumptions:

1. All relevant pricing information, such as the company's history, earnings, assets, and liabilities are factored into a stock's price at all times.
2. Prices move in predictable patterns.
3. Prices tend to move in an upward or downward trend over time.
4. Historical cycles are useful predictors of future market behavior.

Integral to Technical Analysis is the notion of support and resistance, historical limits on the upward and downward price trends. For example, consider a stock that has been priced between $39 at its highest point (the "resistance") and $24 at its lowest (the "support"). When the price falls to $24, the support level, it may be expected to rise. Likewise, when the price reaches $39, it may be expected to fall.

Another trading method, Fundamental Analysis, is predicated on the notion that the faster a company grows, the faster the stock will increase. Examination of earnings and sales are paramount to investment decisions based on this method. Value investing simply means buying a stock at a low price and selling it for more in the future. Growth stocks are stocks issued by a company whose earnings are expected to grow at a predictable rate, or at a faster rate than the market as a whole.

Increasing speculation aimed at rapid turnover and generation of profits led to an increased emphasis on the analysis of external events influencing specific stocks. As an example, assume large purchases of concrete and copper are made by a construction company in Brazil. Recognizing that these commodities are integral to the construction of nuclear energy plants, a trader would invest in stocks of companies involved in nuclear energy construction.

In the current investing environment, human emotions are disproportionately influential, especially when negative events occur. An airplane crash can send airline stocks on a downward spiral, a terrorist attack on a hotel can doom hotel stocks, and a celebrity's choice of clothing at a red carpet event can make or break the stocks of apparel companies.

AI programs used for stock trading may be based on one or all of these methodologies. Some programs are designed only to advise and make recommendations to human traders, whereas the most complex systems have autonomous authority over the buying and selling of stocks, engaging in thousands of transactions per second. Predictive modeling and high-speed transactions, or frequency trading, are the hallmarks of robust AI stock trading programs.

Data Mining in Stock Trading

Over the last three decades, increasingly large amounts of historical data have been stored electronically, and this volume is expected to continue to grow considerably in the future. Data mining is founded on the theory that historical patterns related to buying decisions and behavior will be repeated in the future, 50 percent or more of the time.

Data mining technology is used in stock trading to uncover patterns in price fluctuations and the factors that influence them, with the goal of predicting whether the future price of a particular stock will increase or decrease. The following techniques are widely used in the design of stock trading software: Typical Price (TP), Relative Strength Index (RSI), Chaikin Money Flow Indicator (CMI), Stochastic Momentum Index (SMI), Moving Average (MA), and Text and Data Mining (TDM).

The Typical Price (TP) indicator is produced by calculating the average of the high, low, and closing prices—in other words, by adding them together and dividing by three. The result is the average, or Typical Price. To be useful, the TP must be viewed over a period time, so that upward or downward trends are evident.

A Relative Strength Index (RSI) is a comparison between the number of days on which a stock price is higher or lower at the end of each trading session. Typically, an RSI is computed over a nine-to-fifteen day period. The average number of "up" days is divided by the average number of "down" days, and then added to one. The sum is divided into 100, and the resulted is subtracted from 100. Each RSI has a value ranging between zero and 100. Conventional wisdom suggests that an RSI of 70 or above means a stock has been overbought and is due to decline, whereas an RSI below 30 indicates the price may be about to rise. Typically, the RSI is charted for a period of a year or more to envision the long-term trend.

A Chaikin Money Flow Indicator (CMI) is based on a calculation devised by an investment analyst named Marc Chaikin, comparing accumulation and distribution. If a stock closes above its midpoint for the day, then accumulation is assumed; if it closes below its midpoint, distribution is assumed. The CMI is computed by summing the values of accumulation and distribution for 13 periods and then dividing by the sum of the volume. A high closing price with increasing volume indicates a bullish stock (trending upward). A low closing price with high volume indicates a poor risk. If the CMI is less than zero for an extended period, a downward trend is likely.

The Stochastic Momentum Index (SMI) is based on a technique known as the Stochastic Oscillator. (The term stochastic means a formula based on random values.) The SMI is a comparison between the closing price and the midpoint of the high-low range for the session. The SMI values fall between -100 and +100. When the closing price is greater than the midpoint, the SMI is above zero. When the closing price is less than the midpoint, the SMI is below zero.

Extreme high-low SMI values indicate an overbought condition. A "buy" signal is generated when the SMI rises above -50, or when it crosses above the signal line. A "sell" signal is generated when the SMI falls below +50, or when it crosses below the signal line.

The pricing indicator most commonly used by automated trading systems is the Moving Average (MA). This indicator simply shows the average price of a stock over a period of time, usually 20, 30, 50, 100, or 200 days. When prices fall below the moving average they have a tendency to continue declining. Conversely, when prices rise above the moving average a probable upward trend is signaled.

Text and Data Mining (TDM) is the analysis of data that exists in the form of natural language text, such as journal articles, books, and social media. TDM software enables computers to read and digest digital information far more quickly than a human can. The program breaks down digital information into raw data and text, analyzes it, and forms new connections. Hedge fund managers and stock traders use TDM to mine feeds from sources such as the *Wall Street Journal* and Associated Press to predict the movements of markets.

Long-term forecasts tend to be more predictable than short-term forecasts. One reason, presumably, is that short-term forecasts are more subject to current events, whereas long-term forecasts reflect more fundamental trends.

A popular adage among statisticians is that "if you torture the data long enough, it will confess to anything." In other words, a formula that may seem to apply to the past doesn't necessarily have predictive value for the future. To illustrate this premise, market analyst David Leinweber set out to identify random correlations to Standard and Poor's 500-stock index (the "S&P 500").

The results were described in a *Business Week* article, "He Who Mines Data May Strike Fool's Gold." Leinweber "sifted through a United Nations CD-ROM and discovered that historically, the single best predictor of the Standard & Poor's 500-stock index was butter production in Bangladesh."

Data mining techniques have become significantly more sophisticated—and the body of data to be mined vastly more ponderous—since 1997, when that article was published. Nevertheless, the lesson is equally valid today, for reasons entirely unrelated to either short-term or long-term trends.

Manipulating the Market

Critics of AI trading methods, particularly people employed as investment counselors and brokers, warn that such programs outsmart humans in the financial markets and enable unethical users to instigate market crashes. Such fears are no longer theoretical.

There is a clear separation between traditional trading decisions based on the real or perceived value of the issuing company, and the abstract response to—or outright manipulation of—stock prices for instant gain. In obvious opposition to one another, these contradictory forces continually wage war on a daily basis as the stock market plays out. In this battle, humans are badly outmatched by the machines. AI systems calculate the worth of businesses and make instant buying or selling decisions. Other AI programs are designed to react to price swings and current events.

In the 1960s, each share purchased by an investor was held for an average of four years. Today, that same share is held for 20 seconds. The facilitator of this phenomenon is the rise of high-frequency trading machines capable of executing thousands of transactions in less than a second. An easily visualized peril looms in all this.

An event known to stock traders as "The Flash Crash" is a prime example of the hazards of AI-powered trading. On May 6, 2010, a seemingly normal day on Wall Street, workers in Greece coincidentally began protesting against the country's recently announced austerity measures. With each media report on the crisis, the stock market dipped. The Dow Jones Industrial Average nearly fell 1,000 points and lost $1 trillion, before prices mysteriously began to increase. In the end, the loss shrunk from 1,000 points to 200 points. The entire process took less than ten minutes from start to finish. Amazingly, the crash began as a ripple in the price of e-mini futures contracts traded on the Chicago Mercantile Exchange.

The cause of the shocking Flash Crash has been traced to AI trading machines. As news about the unrest in Greece unraveled, the machines initiated a massive sell-off, creating a lightning-fast downward plunge. The culprits have been identified as rogue investors known as *quants*, Wall Street hackers who intentionally deploy denial-of-service (DoS) attacks aimed at disabling other trading machines. On May 6, 2010, stock market servers became so overloaded that quotes for some shares became delayed by as much as 36 seconds—an eternity compared to the thousands of transactions per second placed by the hackers.

This purposeful disruption of the trading process is referred to as "quote stuffing." In a typical attack, the quants place and cancel random orders 10,000 times per second, or continually step from one share to 100 and back again in a never-ending loop. The stock exchange has internal self-limiting mechanisms designed to halt trading after unnatural price swings; unfortunately, on May 6, they only worked until 2:30 P.M. New York time.

Recent research shows that Flash Crashes are not isolated occurrences, but have occurred quite often over the past century. Of course, there's little risk that even the least ethical abusers will completely bring down the system that rewards their avarice. Extracting wealth, at the expense of the companies they harm, is their *raison d'etre*. Arguably, it is the reason for most trading decisio*ns by humans as well.

Nevertheless, major trading entities, from stock brokerages to retirement funds, have already invested hundreds of millions of dollars in AI technology to optimize their investment decisions, and will continue to do so as long they are allowed. In 2015, a company decided to launch "streams of data from Twitter and the securities discussion site *StockTwits* that are 'normalized' and ready to be fed to computers for analytical processing ...designed for use by hedge funds and high-frequency traders."

The notion of AI controlling the stock market and even all of the financial markets, is no longer regarded as a far-fetched idea, but a normal part of doing business. Regulation of global stock markets is inevitable, with AI-powered controls to prevent abuses and extreme price swings motivated by non-financial influences such as emotional responses to current events.

Should governments fail to implement and enforce such controls, rapidly increasing income disparity and social upheaval will threaten to bring down the very economic systems that sustain them and the people they have vowed to serve.

9

KINDLING THE FLAME

How AI is Changing Education

"Education is the kindling of a flame, not the filling of a vessel."
Socrates

There is a tendency in the academic world to overlook the fact that education is not an end, but a means to an end; it exists in a general sense to enlighten, and in a more specific sense to create an understanding of specific subject matters. Ultimately, education must further the pursuit and expansion of knowledge, cultivate cross-cultural awareness, and help people understand and appreciate natural and human-made systems, processes, and creative endeavors.

In industry, training, as an adjunct to educating, cultivates skills required to perform predefined tasks. Teaching and learning are the fundamental processes of both activities.

Educational techniques have changed little since Plato verbally instructing groups of students in philosophy and language on grassy hillocks of ancient Greece. His most ardent prodigy, Aristotle, carried on the tradition, popularizing education as a normal process, and eventually an institution, of civilization. The two most profound advancements were clearly the invention of the printing press, which gave rise to textbooks, and, more recently, the advent of the computer.

Computer Assisted Instruction

In the 1960s, many researchers began to take advantage of mainframe computers and timesharing to develop computer assisted instructional (CAI) systems. The first digital learning tools were essentially electronic workbooks, with a static "turn-the-page" design, or automated "flash cards." As software became more sophisticated, the systems were able to track student responses and "branch" to varying levels of difficulty and complexity based the individual's progress.

Patrick Suppes and Richard Atkinson at Stanford's Institute for Mathematical Studies in the Social Sciences developed a system that taught reading and arithmetic to elementary school students. In 1967, the researchers founded Computer Curriculum Corporation, which sold complete integrated CAI systems, including hardware and software, to schools.

Around the same time, a system called Programmed Logic for Automatic Teaching Operations (PLATO) was developed at the University of Illinois Urbana-Champaign, featuring a screen that could display both text and graphics. Its integrated programming language, TUTOR, allowed teachers to build their own automated lessons.

Advancements in computer-assisted instruction continued throughout the 1970s and 1980s. The merger of behavior science learning techniques with logic-based AI systems transformed teaching machines from mere automated workbooks into adaptive tutors. This new breed of intelligent teaching systems accelerated the learning of computer applications, applied sciences, industrial design, and engineering. AI programming languages also made it possible to build accurate simulations of complex environments for use in teaching and training in aerospace, astronomy, geology, oceanography, and even biological systems.

Adaptive Teaching Systems

As the field of cognitive science has advanced, so has research in educational technology. Artificial Intelligence in education and training is currently focused on three aspects: analysis, delivery, and assessment.

Instructional analysis is the process of determining what the contents of a specific curriculum, course, and teaching method should be.

Delivery is made up of the hardware and software required to teach or train specified subject matters.

Assessment is the process of evaluating the extent to which learning has actually occurred—in effect, validating the instructional analysis and delivery method.

A cornerstone of the development of AI-empowered computer tutors is the ability to personalize the teaching of a specific subject matter, while allowing students to learn at their own pace. Research has shown that a majority of students may be more comfortable interacting with a computer in a learning situation than in a competitive classroom setting, where they routinely risk "punishment" by humiliation.

The efforts to create self-teaching ("autotutorial") machines actually date back to the 1950s. Even the earliest teaching machines made of typewriter parts were intended to be "adaptive." The underlying objective has remained the same, as expressed by psychologist B. F. Skinner in 1958:

> *"The machine itself, of course, does not teach. It simply brings the student into contact with the person who composed the material it presents. It is a laborsaving device because it can bring one programmer into contact with an indefinite number of students. This may suggest mass production, but the effect upon each student is surprisingly like that of a private tutor."*

Indeed, throughout history personal tutors have been valued by people in diverse walks of life, both rich and poor, as a presumably superior alternative to classroom instruction. Royalty and the rich have provided their children with private tutoring, but home schooling by parents must also be considered in this category. Just as a private tutor directs all its attention to a singular pupil, crafting each lesson for that student based on his or her aptitude and pace of learning, an autotutorial system personalizes the learning experience and adapts its delivery for each learner.

A skilled human tutor keeps the student focused and motivated, by exercising expertise, teaching skill, encouragement, and compassion. The student interacts with the tutor by asking questions or changing the topic. In short, a tutored student is a more active and engaged learner.

Benjamin Bloom, a psychologist specializing in learning behavior, published the findings of a study conducted in 1984, showing "the average student under tutoring was about two standard deviations above the average" of a conventional classroom consisting of one teacher and 30 students. Despite this controversial indictment of public and private schools, Bloom admitted that one-on-one tutoring is "too costly for most societies to bear on a large scale."

Computer tutors hold the promise of invalidating that premise—not just in the households of the elite and eclectic, but also in traditional classrooms.

Robots in the Classroom

Not all AI-equipped teaching devices are designed for private tutoring. Classroom robots are presently the focus of widespread research and increasing deployment in schools.

Brian David Johnson, the designer of an open-source, programmable humanoid robot, insists that robotic teachers are the future of elementary education. He believes that "inherently, education is about people, but robots can be excellent extensions of parents and teachers at home and in the classroom." One reason for their acceptance, he maintains, is that "robots inhabit our imaginations."

For children with different learning styles or learning disabilities, robots have the potential to excel as teachers or learning companions. Like a private tutor, a robot can give an individual child unfettered attention. "Unlike computers or tablets, robots are social and can connect with children," Johnson insists.

A robot named RUBI, developed by the University of California at San Diego, currently teaches foreign languages to preschoolers in California. Robosem, developed by Yujin Robot, teaches English to Korean students. The robot can teleconference with a human instructor or administer pre-loaded, autonomous lessons using motion tracking and speech recognition software.

In Birmingham, England, a robot named Nao teaches autistic children. With no concept of psychological barriers or awkward behavior, Nao is able to teach without creating negative reactions.

On the elementary school level, classroom robots are mostly deployed for very specific repetitive tasks, such as vocabulary, attendance and behavior imitation. AI enables the robot to learn as it teaches, by detecting signals that capture the attention of young children.

In an Australian study conducted by the Latitude consulting group in association with the LEGO Learning Institute and Project Synthesis, students from ages eight to twelve in Australia, France, Germany, South Africa, the United Kingdom, and the United States imagined robots as better versions of their parents and teachers, willing to take on mundane tasks so that the child could focus on higher-level pursuits. Thirty-eight percent of the children wanted a robot to teach them, while thirty-eight percent wanted a robot to play with them.

The study showed that in-classroom robots promote learning and creativity because children see technology as fundamentally "human." In their answers, children describe their robot as patient, reassuring, and supportive. Most of the children in the study thought their robots demonstrated qualities that they would like to emulate. Many felt that robots inspired them to be creative.

The most important information to be gleaned from the Australian study is that children are most likely to be receptive to robots in classrooms.

A classroom robot must be able to fulfill the following requirements:

1. It must be an expert in its subject matter, either by means of its engineered knowledge base, machine learning ability, or both.

2. It must be able to account for student errors, not merely indicate whether an answer is correct or incorrect.

3. It must be able to assess how the student works to solve a problem.

4. It must provide feedback.

5. It must be able to adjust to an individual student's aptitudes and cultural traits.

6. It must be able to recognize questions asked by the student and provide an appropriate response.

Once considered formidable, or even impossible, creating such behavior by a machine, whether an autotutorial computer program or a classroom robot, is presently feasible. Acceptance is a separate issue.

From the time CAI programs were first offered to schools and training centers, resistance by faculty members became evident. A notion popular among teachers and trainers was that, if successful, autotutorial technology would obsolete human instructors in the classroom. That resistance, which still persists today, was perhaps the main reason educational technology has not yet realized its full potential.

Brian David Johnson, author of *21st Century Robot*, reassures teachers that the goal of ITS is to supplement, not replace, human student-teacher interaction. “Inherently, education is about people," he wrote, "but robots can be excellent extensions of parents and teachers at home and in the classroom." In Johnson's view, for children with different learning styles or learning disabilities, robots can be excellent teachers and learning companions. A robotic tutor can give a child undivided attention, in contrast to a teacher confronting a classroom of students.

Nevertheless, there are situations in which machine-based learning is demonstrably more efficient and cost-effective, especially in business and industry.

AI in Industrial Training

According to the American Society for Training and Development (ASTD), annual spending by corporations on employee training represents about two percent of total payroll dollars. Increasingly, management looks to intelligent training systems to increase effectiveness, efficiency and overall return on investment. The same Intelligent Tutoring Systems (ITS) technology used in schoolrooms is capable of creating not just trained novices, but content experts. These systems provide intelligent, individualized coaching, performance assessment, and feedback, activities needed for students to acquire broad and deep expertise.

Computer-based simulations let students "learn by doing," replicating on-the-job situations. Pioneered by the aviation industry and the military, simulations are being adopted by more and more businesses to help trainees learn diverse subjects such as equipment and software operations and maintenance, business and analytical skills, and interpersonal skills. An essential feature of a robust simulation environment is the use of intelligent tutoring to provide coaching during exercises, assess the trainee's performance, and produce meaningful feedback. In this setting, AI training technologies have been shown to be very effective.

An ITS program assesses each learner's actions as the instruction takes place and develops a model of his or her knowledge, skills, and learning pace. Instructional strategies are then tailored based on the learner model. Research using intelligent tutoring in industrial settings indicates that employees generally learn more quickly and demonstrate improved job performance after training.

In the 1980s, researchers at Carnegie Mellon University developed an intelligent tutoring system called the LISP Tutor to teach computer programming. Students who were taught by the ITS scored 43 percent higher on the final exam than a control group that received traditional instruction. When given complex programming problems, the control group required 30 percent more time to solve these problems, compared to the ITS students.

Another ITS, called Sherlock, was developed in the early 1990s to train Air Force personnel on jet aircraft trouble-shooting procedures. Learners taught using Sherlock performed significantly better than the control group and, after 20 hours of instruction, performed as well as technicians with four years of on-the-job experience.

Since then, tutorial technology has spread in both university and industrial settings.

Intelligent tutoring consists of three phases: student modeling, expert modeling, and instructor modeling.

Student modeling is used to determine the student's knowledge, skills, and other attributes that affect how the student should be taught.

During *expert modeling*, the subject matter expertise is engineered, along with any appropriate simulations and heuristics used by experts in the field to solve problems.

Instructor modeling provides the specific methodology that will be used based on the student model.

A variety of artificial intelligence (AI) techniques are used to capture how a problem can be solved. For example, some ITS systems capture subject matter expertise in rules. This structure enables the tutoring system to generate problems on the fly and assess learners' understanding by comparing their reasoning and problem-solving processes with those used by the expert system.

By referring to the student model of the student's strengths and weaknesses, the ITS can provide carefully selected instruction and practice opportunities to optimize learning conditions. When simulations are used, the tutoring system can analyze the learner's actions and estimate his or her knowledge gains and skills.

The instructor model is designed to encode instructional methods that are appropriate for both the subject matter and the learner. For example, if a student has been assessed as a novice, the instructor module would begin with a lower level of instruction but offer a higher level of coaching.

As ITS technology evolved, it expanded, predictably, onto the internet.

In 2012, the Massachusetts Institute of Technology launched the first in a series of fully automated online courses. Known as MITx, the internet delivery system replicates traditional courses offered by the university, with virtual laboratories, e-textbooks, online discussions, and videotaped lectures. The flagship course, *6.002x: Circuits and Electron-*

ics, is based on the campus-based course with the same title. Other planned content included automated versions of biology, math, and physics courses.

It is inevitable that, in the not-so-distant future, completely automated online universities will deliver academic and vocational content to learners in their homes, using individualized self-paced instruction and automated assessment techniques.

Resistance to Change

Intelligent training systems face the same level and type of resistance as the evolving ITS technologies currently making their ways into schools. Industrial and corporate trainers, like their counterparts in academia, are fearful of losing their livelihoods if the implementation of automated teaching machines proves successful.

Human opposition is presently the biggest obstacle to the adoption of intelligent learning systems in both the public and private sectors. As Leonardo Da Vinci said, "it is easier to resist at the beginning than at the end."

The Aristotelian concept of education—lecturing to a flock of spellbound students—is a romantic ideal hard to dismiss. Indeed, human interaction will, and should, be an intractable component of the academic experience as long as academic institutions exist.

10

FIRE AND FORGET

How AI is Changing War

"Whereas the short-term impact of AI depends on who controls it, the long-term impact depends on whether it can be controlled at all."
Stephen Hawking

In a 2015 memorandum to the Defense Science Board, Undersecretary of Defense Frank Kendall announced the development of a military roadmap for Artificial Intelligence. In the Undersecretary's words, the emphasis will be on "exploration of the bounds — both technological and social — that limit the use of autonomy across a wide range of military operations." The project will seek the answers to such questions as:

> *"What activities cannot today be performed autonomously? When is human intervention required? What limits the use of autonomy? How might we overcome those limits and expand the use of autonomy in the near term as well as over the next two decades?"*

The memorandum referred to IBM's question-and-answer machine, Watson, the use of robotics and automation, self-driving vehicles, intelligent supply chain management, and other applications.

At precisely 7:47 A.M. on May 17, 2017, the robotic X-37B Orbital Test Vehicle touched down at the Shuttle Landing Facility at NASA's Kennedy Space Center, after 718 days in space. It was the fourth and longest mission completed by the U.S. Air Force space plane. The first mission, which launched in April 2010, lasted 225 days. Exactly what the self-flying spaceship did during all that time logged in orbit remains a mystery.

Theories about the aircraft's mission range from spying on foreign countries to reconnaissance for bombing missions. Observers keeping a watch on the space plane reported that it passed over the same area of the planet every four days, lending credence to the spy mission theory.

Equip the X-37B with a space cannon, self-guided missiles, or nuclear devices, and the robot plane instantly becomes a space weapon of unprecedented versatility and destructive capability.

The New Weapons Race

Recent decades have witnessed the feverish development of robotic weaponry, vehicles, and drones designed specifically for military applications. The U.S. Army has been deploying semi-autonomous robots in combat zones for reconnaissance and bomb defusal since 2000. Thousands of tactical robots were unleashed on Iraq and Afghanistan. Eventually, the Pentagon plans to replace human soldiers with robots and autonomous weapons altogether. The benefits are obvious: why subject humans to the dangers and suffering of war, if machines are able to perform their missions without risk to human life?

South Korea has aggressively pursued the commercial development of autonomous weaponry for sale to the highest bidder. The Korean-made Super aEgis II self-guided gun turret is able to identify, track, and destroy targets without any guidance or assistance from a human. Unlike human snipers, the Super aEgis II never sleeps, can see in the dark, and virtually never misses its prey. The turret is currently deployed in numerous locations in the Middle East and at military bases around the world.

In 2013, the Russian Republic announced plans to expand its use of robotic weaponry, christening new production and research facilities. The Russian-made Platform-M is a remote controlled robotic unit on a crawler, armed with grenade launchers and Kalashnikov rifles. The unit is designed "for gathering intelligence, for discovering and eliminating stationary and mobile targets, for firepower support, for patrolling and for guarding important sites. The unit's weapons can be guided, it can carry out supportive tasks and it can destroy targets in automatic or semiautomatic control systems."

Platform-M is equipped with optical-electronic and radio reconnaissance locators, which enable the killing machine to perform combat tasks in darkness. The Armata combat tank, unveiled in 2015, is fully robotic-capable and, according to the Russian government, equipped with more fire power than the robot tanks developed by Western nations.

The Harpy drone deployed by the Israeli military is an example of a "fire and forget" autonomous weapon. A winged guided missile, the drone hovers over an area until it identifies a target and then decides by itself whether to attack. The Harpy is currently used to detect and destroy enemy radar installations, though modifications to its programming could theoretically arm it for any type of "fire and forget" mission.

One of the first efforts by the U.S. to incorporate artificial intelligence with weaponry was a robotic land mine, with computer vision and sensors capable of detecting minute vibrations. Self-learning software enabled the mines to detect and distinguish between objects such as humans, vehicles, animals, or debris. The prototype was equipped with mechanical legs, making it a robot as well as a mine, theoretically able to move out of the way of a noncombatant, or directly into the path of an unaware enemy.

Qinetiq North America currently manufactures miniature three-foot long robot tanks capable of moving rapidly over diverse terrain on caterpillar tracks, destroying targets with devastating accuracy.

Besides roaming battlebots, entire fleets of unmanned air, sea, and land vehicles are currently in use by militaries around the world. With more than 90 countries as customers, the robotic weapons industry promises to be produce $98 billion in revenues over the next eight years, with the United States the biggest buyer.

Qinetiq's tanks presently rely on human soldiers for remote control and are limited in range to about 2,600 feet. The technology already exists to make the units—or similar rivals—capable of functioning independently without human control.

In June of 2016, Israel Aerospace Industries unveiled the RoBattle unmanned ground vehicle, capable of operating independently or as a support unit for convoy protection, ambush, attack, or reconnaissance. Six wheels with independent suspension allow the robot vehicle to scale obstacles, such as rubble and small walls, and multiple sensors enable it to identify images in daylight or darkness.

Robotic boats developed by the U.S. Navy are designed to swarm an enemy vessel like sharks circling their prey, as part of a comprehensive plan to deploy surface, underwater, and flying robotic vehicles. The boats are commanded by a system called the Control Architecture for Robotic Agent Command and Sensing (CARACaS), which not only steers the autonomous vehicles but also coordinates their actions with other boats in a larger group of vessels, both manned and unmanned. CARACaS evolved from hardware and software originally used in NASA's Mars rover program starting in 2005.

Each robot boat transmits its radar views to the others, so that the group shares the same situational awareness. They also continually compute their own courses to navigate around obstacles in cooperation with other boats in the swarm. Such robotic swarm technology could transform modern warfare for the military by reducing the risk to human personnel.

A larger robot ship, the Anti-Submarine Warfare Continuous Trail Unmanned Vessel (ACTUV), was developed to track enemy submarines in shallow waters. The ACTUV is capable of operating autonomously for 60 to 90 days without interruption, surveiling large stretches of ocean territory.

If an enemy submarine is detected, the autonomous vessel will guide other ships to the target's location, to confront and destroy the hostile vessel. The ACTUV prototype, dubbed the Sea Hunter, is presently unarmed.

Eventually, The Pentagon intends to make its Predator drones that are now used in combat fully autonomous—in other words, free to identify and destroy targets on their own, without any guidance or interference from a human. Self-driving tanks and battle trucks are already a reality. Even the self-driving cars being tested on streets and highways today

The U.S. Navy's prototype robot submarine, the Sea Hunter, capable of operating autonomously for up to 90 days.

were spawned by a competition sponsored by the U.S. Department of Defense.

It is impossible to discuss artificial intelligence in any context—military, industrial, or scientific—without acknowledging the Defense Advanced Research Projects Agency, commonly known by its acronym DARPA.

DARPA

From the internet to GPS, the U.S. Defense Department's research and development arm is responsible for some of the world's most significant scientific and technological breakthroughs.

In 1957, when America's Cold War enemy the Soviet Union launched the first human-engineered satellite into orbit, the U.S. government was caught by surprise. In response, President Dwight D. Eisenhower authorized the Advanced Research Projects Agency, the predecessor to DARPA, with a mission to formulate and execute research and development projects to expand the frontiers of technology and science, with initial funding of $520 million, at the time a vast sum.

Initially, the agency focused on space exploration and ballistic missile defense. DARPA acquired its present name in 1972 and began to explore energy production, information technology, and military applications.

The list of DARPA projects past and present reads like a litany of science fiction plots: killer robots, brain chips, self-aware computers.

The agency's subsequent technological achievements included tactical armor and anti-armor programs, infrared sensing for space-based surveillance, high-energy laser technology for space-based missile defense, antisubmarine warfare, cruise missiles, advanced aircraft, and computing innovations aimed at gaining military advantages over potential enemies. The agency's continuing research into integrated circuits resulted in the technology behind Very Large Scale Integration (VLSI) and charged particle beams.

Recently, DARPA 's Fast Lightweight Autonomy (FLA) program resulted in the development of a tiny flying drone capable of navigating corridors at just 45 MPH without human guidance. The lightweight device was equipped with a high-definition camera and numerous onboard sensors, enabling it to distinguish and avoid obstacles.

During a military operation, natural disaster, or other deployment scenario, the drone could be released into a building through a window to provide video surveillance of the entire interior.

One of DARPA's current missions is to integrate biology, engineering, and computer science to produce breakthroughs in research, discovery, and applications for the benefit of national security. Robotic systems, advanced prosthetics, brain-machine interfaces, innovative manufacturing technologies, adaptable sensor systems, computing platforms, and countermeasures for biological agents all fall into this category.

Machine Learning

In 2013, DARPA launched Probabilistic Programming for Advancing Machine Learning (PPAML), in search of rapid advancements in machine learning. The project's goal is to make machine learning capability more accessible and effective for a wide variety of military weapons and information systems. Using probabilistic programming to increase the number of people who can build machine learning applications, DARPA plans to make such experts more effective and enable new applications literally unimaginable using today's technology.

Examples of machine learning include self-driving vehicles, image search and activity detection, object tracking, topic models, "spam" filters, expert systems, predictive databases, and gene sequencing. Although enabling computers to learn from their experiences can be valuable, building effective machine learning applications today requires Herculean efforts on the part of experts.

In 2015, scientists at New York University developed an algorithm that captures the learning abilities of humans, enabling a computer to recognize and draw visual concepts in exactly the same way as a person. According to the team leader, Brenden Lake, the advancement dramatically shortens the time it takes a computer to learn new concepts and broadens the machine's ability to perform more creative tasks.

A human exposed to a new concept, such as a new dance move or a symbol on a sign, often needs only a few examples to develop an understanding. While machines can now perform some pattern-recognition tasks such as reading an address on an envelope, they typically need to consult hundreds or thousands of examples to perform with accuracy. To date, building a computer that requires as little data as a human when learning a new concept has escaped the grasp of hardware and software designers.

The NYU researchers set out to shorten the learning process and make it more akin to the way humans acquire and apply knowledge, by learning from a small number of examples and performing a range of tasks, such as generating new examples of a concept or generating entirely new concepts. Before they get to kindergarten, children learn to recognize new concepts from just a single example, and can even imagine new examples they haven't seen.

To mimic human learning, the research team developed a so-called Bayesian Program Learning (BPL) framework, in which concepts are represented as simple computer programs. For instance, the letter A is represented by a program that generates examples of the letter when the code is run.

We are still far from building machines as smart as a human child, but the NYU project demonstrated for the first time that a machine is capable of learning and using a large class of real-world concepts in a manner similar to humans.

Also in 2015, DARPA launched a five-year plan to develop implants that could monitor the human brain, and created a program called Systems-Based Neurotechnology for Emerging Therapies (SUBNETS). The project will investigate therapies that use near real-time recording, analysis, and stimulation in next-generation devices inspired by current deep brain stimulation (DBS), which involves implanting electrodes within specific areas of the brain.

According to DARPA, the SUBNETS project will result in an innovative neurotechnological therapy to produce major improvements in the quality of life of patients suffering from mental disorders, especially for service members and veterans who have very few options with existing therapies. DARPA is also a major participant in the Brain Research through Advancing Innovative Neurotechnologies (BRAIN) initiative, which is engaged in research to better understand and map the human brain.

The present and future benefits of DARPA research in all these fields can be neither denied nor ignored. Nevertheless, the reality of automated machine guns capable of finding, tracking, and eliminating human targets, absent of human guidance, already exists in our world. The technology behind self-driving cars is already being applied to self-guided drones. A fully autonomous Predator drone will decide based on its fuzzy logic whether to fire on a house whose occupants include both enemy soldiers and civilians. The crucial issue faced by civilization as a whole is how to assure that such devices arrive at the right decision.

Not to be left behind in the race for AI supremacy, NASA created the Quantum Artificial Intelligence Laboratory, or QuAIL, to assess the potential of quantum computers to perform calculations too difficult for conventional super-computers. NASA's goal is to utilize quantum computing to improve a wide range of tasks that can lead to world-changing discoveries and technologies.

Quantum computing is based on quantum bits or *qubits*. Unlike traditional computers, in which bits must have a value of either zero or one, a qubit can represent a zero, a one, or both values simultaneously. Representing data in qubits allows information to be processed in ways that are beyond the capability of a traditional computer using binary ones and zeros to represent data. Theoretically, a quantum computer could be capable of analyzing and solving, within a matter of a few days, extremely complex problems that would take a traditional computer millions of years.

Military Nanotechnology

DARPA and NASA aren't the only government initiatives charged with producing world-changing developments based on artificial intelligence. In 2001, the National Nanotechnology Initiative (NNI) was created, with the mission of achieving technological supremacy in the field of molecule-sized weapons development. The NNI is the U.S. Government's interagency program for coordinating research and development, and enhancing communication and collaborative activities, in nanoscale science, engineering, and technology. The world's major military players are heavily involved in research and development of nanotechnology, especially military applications.

Nanorobots, whether synthetic or biological, are able to function on a molecular level to perform preprogrammed tasks such as injecting RNA into cells, removing sclerotic plaques from arteries, and repairing heart valves.

The Department of Defense has developed a new class of weaponry based on nanotechnology: powerful miniature bombs, using nanometals, such as nanoaluminum, to create ultra-high burn rate chemical explosives more powerful than conventional bombs. Nanothermite or "superthermite" is one example of such a "Metastable Intermolecular Composite" (MIC.)

The goal of some scientists is to create a completely mechanical, autonomous nanorobot. The technology currently exists to create self-replicating assembly robots to build entire arsenals of advanced nanoweapons, or fleets of microscopic attack robots, in the same way a virus such as influenza or Ebola replicates itself.

The raw computational power made possible by nanotechnology will lead to previously unanticipated advancements in the development of artificial intelligence applications. Advanced molecular manufacturing capabilities will eventually determine the future balance of power between nations.

Nanofactory-level molecular nanotechnology could bring between 100 to 1,000,000-fold increases in military capabilities. Clearly, nations lacking a molecular manufacturing ability will be at the mercy of their enemies.

An algorithm that today requires a large supercomputer to execute will be possible to run onboard a bullet or fit into an insect-sized nanorobot. Smart dust and other nanocomputer-enabled systems can be linked together on the battlefield by means of localized computer networks. An army of self-replicating nanorobots would surpass nuclear weapons in destructiveness, requiring only a single speck made of ordinary elements to destroy all life.

Ironically, to build a defense against an offensive weapon equipped with artificial intelligence or nanotechnology requires envisioning such a weapon in precise detail. A civilization that persists in the never-ending pursuit of newer and more effective means of exacting human suffering and planetary destruction will ultimately succeed, on an unimaginably horrific scale.

11

NOT WITH A BANG BUT A WHIMPER

How AI is Changing Civilization

"The end of the human race will be that it will eventually die of civilization."
Ralph Waldo Emerson

Dismissing superintelligent machines as mere science fiction "would be a mistake, and potentially our worst mistake ever," according to celebrated Cambridge University physicist Stephen Hawking, who suffers from motor neurone disease and relies on AI software to communicate. He, along with notable entrepreneurs such as Bill Gates and Elon Musk, intellectuals such as Noam Chomsky and Max Tegman, and over 1,000 other scientists and educators (including the author of this book), have expressed concern that the current fervent development of AI may lead ultimately to the extinction of humanity. In a letter presented to the Artificial Intelligence Conference in Brazil in 2015, on behalf of the Future of Life Institute, the cosigners advocated researching the existential risks and ethical concerns associated with the rapid onset of superintelligent AI.

While many sensationalist opinions have appeared in published and social media, it is important to pay attention to certain key points made in the previous chapters of this book:

The AI arms race is already underway. It is impossible at this point to prevent the continued research, development, and deployment of autonomous weapons capable of mass destruction and human suffering on a global scale. Virtually every government, militant group, and terror monger will eventually have access to "Killer AI."

Continued advancements in machine intelligence may result in computers that are able to research, design, engineer, and produce even more intelligent computers. Those super-intelligent machines could have programming and capabilities we humans may not even be able to understand, much less control.

AI fused with nanotechnology can be used to create swarms of lethal pathogens, both natural and artificial, against which there is no possible defense.

It is the nature of enterprises, including technology companies, to "race to the bottom," maximizing profits by minimizing costs. Conspicuously, the cost of designing and incorporating security safeguards against hacker attacks, sabotage, terrorism, and other inevitable hazards are routinely omitted in the design, engineering, and manufacturing of AI-empowered devices.

Technology-related job losses in industrialized countries, unless mitigated by governments and employers, will result in extreme wealth inequality, spurring increased social upheaval, mass migration, crime, and civil unrest.

Increased dependence on technology will make civilization as a whole vulnerable to sudden collapse as a result of numerous causes, including sabotage, depletion of available resources, and adverse natural phenomena such as solar storms and climate events.

By now, as I stated at the beginning of this book, thinking machine chaos may already be inevitable. Most likely it will occur not as a sudden explosion of out-of-control autonomous devices, but as a phenomenon that makes its way into everyday life, much in the same methodical way as natural disasters resulting from climate change. T. S. Elliot mused that the world will end "not with a bang but a whimper." Though overreliance on emergent technologies may not end the world, it will unavoidably complicate and challenge human existence.

Risks of AI

In 2016, the Institute for Business Value conducted a study to determine how business leaders and managers view the advent of AI in the workplace. The results revealed that 95 percent of managers familiar with AI technology believe that AI will play a disruptive role in commerce. Furthermore, 75 percent believe it will critically affect the future of their organizations. A full 98 percent of the companies surveyed intend to invest in cognitive computing in the near future.

The most realistic risks associated with the widespread proliferation of AI-empowered devices are basic mistakes, breakdowns and cyber attacks. Consumer products that use fuzzy logic and sensors are far more energy-efficient than those manufactured in the past. For example, a modern refrigerator uses half the energy of one that was made fifteen years ago. Unfortunately, the increasing use of digital technology and soft AI has rendered such products more vulnerable to breakage.

According to *Consumer Reports*, 36 percent of side-by-side refrigerator/freezers with icemakers need to be replaced or repaired within three to four years. Fully one in four front-loading washing machines and one in five dishwashers break down in the same span. Breakdowns of products laden with electronics are more likely to be catastrophic, as well.

Product quality is a function of manufacturing cost, the economic environment, and corporate profits. The ever-increasing drive to maximum profits by minimizing production costs has already led the majority of U.S. firms to establish or contract with overseas facilities, especially in China, to manufacture consumer products. Contractors lure corporate customers by keeping design costs low and engineering services low. As a result, there is a tendency to focus on profitability rather than the interests of the consumer. Companies continually respond to competition by releasing new products, to the detriment of design, engineering, manufacturing, and especially testing.

Thomas Dietterich, professor of computer science at Oregon State University, is concerned that the enormously complex algorithms may not always work as intended. The most imminent threats, Dietterich believes, are cyber attacks conducted using AI software.

If the world's military powers achieve their goal of replacing human soldiers with autonomous weapons, future wars will be waged by machines that, by themselves, without human intervention, will make the decision when, where, and whom to kill. When rogue nations and terror groups gain access to autonomous killing machines, the human suffering and economic impact will almost certainly multiply. It is not unthinkable that humans and the killing machines of their own making could end up in a devastating war against each other.

The development of nanobots capable of rearranging atoms could replicate the ribosome factory that resides within human cells, reading information encoded in DNA to assemble the building blocks of biological life.

Australian researcher Hugo de Garis has predicted that, within a single generation, it will "very probably be possible to store a single bit of information on a single atom". Such a development would allow a disc-sized object to hold a trillion terabits of data, dwarfing the 23 million bits of information a human brain is capable of storing.

The resulting technology could very well lead to the creation of machines vastly superior to our own brains. De Garis warns that, by the end of the 21st century, there could be a war between humanity and intelligent machines.

Even the most seemingly helpful and benign AI developments have significant risks. For example, literally any device connected to the internet, whether a self-driving car or a self-regulating thermostat, can be hacked, creating a virtual open door to sabotage. It has been demonstrated repeatedly that cars with built-in internet connections can be sabotaged by anyone holding a cell phone.

Societal and Cultural Risks

There are societal and cultural challenges associated with commercial AI development, as well. Among the people employed in the transportation industry who will lose their jobs to self-driving trucks and trains, inevitably some will strive to sabotage their vehicular enemies at every possible turn. Inevitable chip failures and circuit problems will cause self-driving cars to race amok, break down, and crash. As of this writing, enough U.S. states have already banned self-driving vehicles to make coast-to-coast shipments by autonomous trucks economically infeasible. It is predictable that many politicians and their constituents will vigorously oppose self-driving vehicles, on the basis of potential job losses, safety, security, and financial incentives from companies that stand to lose market share.

In the near future, nearly every type of household device or appliance will be available as a "connected" component of the Internet of Things. Privacy safeguards for such devices are presently so poor that a rogue search engine has been created to allow voyeurs to observe infants in their cribs via the internet-connected security cameras installed by the parents. Autonomous thermostats currently used in thousands of homes can cause the entire electrical system to fail when they crash.

Though thinking machine chaos may be inevitable, much of the hand wringing over the pace of AI research is based on a more fundamental existential issue. Rather than creating faster calculating machines, research into cognitive computing focuses on creating devices that can interpret their environment and modify themselves accordingly—in other words, the machine equivalent of a self-aware being. This new AI species might rapidly re-engineer itself to produce weapons, biological systems, and other technologies beyond the comprehension of humans.

One of the most highly publicized concerns is that such advanced computers could become disdainful of humans and take steps to drive humanity to extinction—not simply because the machines are more intelligent and efficient, but because it is their mission to optimize life on earth. From a purely logical perspective, eliminating humans would be, if not the first, the most essential step toward such an end. Nick Bostrom's parable of the paper clip factory (described in Chapter Two) is perhaps the most sensationalist example.

"Before the prospect of an intelligence explosion," the philosophy professor wrote, fretfully, "we humans are like small children playing with a bomb. We have little idea when the detonation will occur, though if we hold the device to our ear we can hear a faint ticking sound."

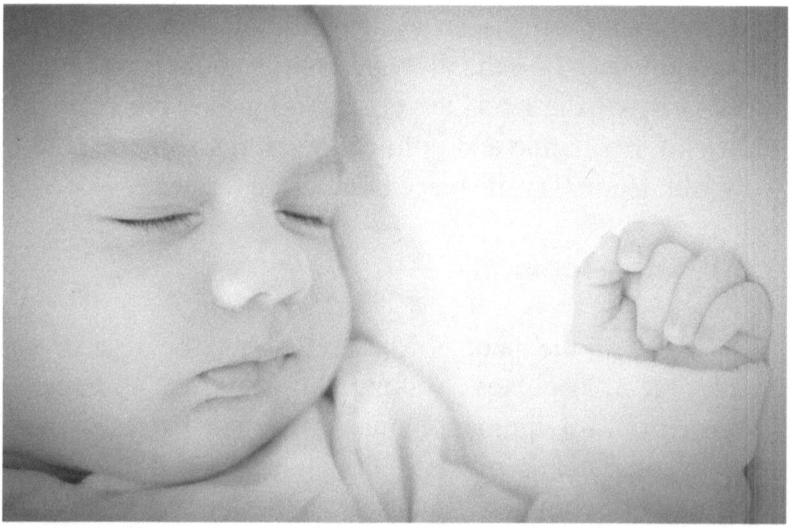

A rogue search engine enabled voyeurs to view infants in their cribs via hacked internet-connected security cameras.

Ray Kurzweil, a pop-science author who, as of this writing, is employed as a spokesperson for Google, has predicted that by 2029, machine intelligence will equal that of humans, and that, by 2045, computers will be a billion times more intelligent than all of the human brains on earth combined. He opines that when brainy computers become smarter than humans, there will be an "intelligence explosion" that will radically change civilization.

Among academicians, Nick Bostrom is the perhaps the best known philosophy professor worrying about the extinction of humanity at the hands of artificial intelligence. It should be noted that neither Ray Kurweil nor Nick Bostrom has written a single AI computer program. Of course, that fact doesn't disqualify either of them from expressing their concerns as educators or computer company spokespersons.

Even if the superintelligent machine-human species they visualize is never actualized, AI could still have enormous destabilizing effects on society. Robots that are now being developed and on the drawing boards could replace the vast majority of the labor force, spawning massive political upheaval. Economic and political pressures could lead to huge wealth inequality, displacement, and even war.

AI Risk Assessment

Most of the people who fret about the rise of superintelligent machines "waking up" as sensient beings and setting out to eliminate humanity are not AI researchers, or even computer scientists—but philosophy and math teachers, captains of commerce, and science fiction writers. Computer scientists tend to have a more balanced, reason-based view.

The dystopian pop-science vision of AI equates intelligence with autonomy—the notion that if a machine acquires the attributes of human intelligence, it will also acquire free will. Philosophically, the concept may seem feasible, but there is no technical basis for even postulating such a possibility. Most AI researchers consider the idea of computers that could someday re-invent, update, and enhance themselves to create a sensient AI "species" to be fanciful.

Virtually all of the speculation aimed at such goals is theoretical. The bitter truth—or, depending on one's perspective, the good news—is that imagining something does not necessarily make it possible. One has only to look at the vast body of mythology and pseudo-scientific whim throughout history to realize this is so. Nevertheless, it is essential to conceptualize a hazard in order to safeguard against it.

It is fundamentally important to realize that scientific breakthroughs leading to technological innovations require enormous resources—mainly, substantial funding as well as exceptional minds. By definition, both types of resources are in relatively short supply. Competition for resources often spawns exaggerated and sometimes sensationalist claims. Companies striving to promote new technologies that are currently in the planning process or in the infancy of development are especially susceptible to exaggeration. Press releases for supposedly "groundbreaking" products in speech and image recognition, virtual reality, and deep learning applications seem to flood the news on a daily basis, in a never-ending quest for financing and stock sales.

In 1965, Gordon Moore, an executive at Fairchild Semiconductor, wrote that "the complexity for minimum component costs (of circuit boards) has increased at a rate of roughly a factor of two per year." Ten years later, a lecturer at California Institute of Technology referred to the notion that the number of transistors on a printed circuit board would increase twofold every year forever as "Moore's Law."

Though Moore denied that he ever considered this speculation to be some sort of immutable scientific law, the term persisted in popular usage. Moore's whimsical "law" has been repeatedly invoked by publicity-seeking writers to "prove" that the rise of hyper-intelligent machines capable of re-inventing themselves into a sensient superspecies is inevitable.

It needs to be emphasized that cheerleading for an inevitability is *per se* nonsensical. If something is inevitable, it will happen whether or not anyone cheers for it. Arguing intensely to convince others of the inevitability of a thing is an indicator of self-interest or self-aggrandizement.

Perhaps the biggest irony of the quest for superintelligence is that, in terms of biological evolution, it is impossible to prove that intelligence is of positive adaptive value for the long-term survival of a species. Intelligence enabled humans to thrive, develop advanced weapons, cultivate and share knowledge, extend longevity, give form to creative expression, and reach out to the stars. However, on the calendar of biological life, humans and their civilization have existed for mere seconds—and on the geological clock, just nanoseconds.

Dinosaurs dominated the earth for much longer periods than us. Plants, birds, even insects, have existed and thrived more successfully than humans and for a longer time. Viewed from the moment of the emergence of life to the present, intelligence is a microscopic blip, no more than random noise. Already, humanity is on the verge of extinction from any number of catastrophes engineered by its own intelligence.

Ironically, the quest for superintelligent machines, at least in theory, holds the potential to either hasten or prevent that extinction.

12

THE MESSAGES GOING OVER THE WIRES

How to Design a Human Brain

"What turns the gears in our brains isn't information, but ideas, inventions, and inspiration."
Clifford Stoll

The term Artificial Intelligence is used in a number of different contexts, not all of which are related to the notion of sentient machines. The animated "virtual assistants" that answer questions on websites are based on programming that their designers refer to as artificial intelligence. Likewise, the data-mining scripts that pry deep into the data stored on the PCs, tablets, and smartphones of internet users are considered artificial intelligence by their implementers. The fuzzy logic that tells a clothes dryer when to shut off based on heat sensor readings is also considered artificial intelligence by appliance manufacturers.

The popular notion of AI molded by cinema and fiction is far more adventurous and, from a programmer's perspective, vastly more complicated. Yet, the premise of creating an artificial human brain remains, if not the most reachable, certainly the most glamorous technological quest now underway. To understand the nature and scope of this challenge, you must truly appreciate the astonishing architecture of the human brain.

Our brains are each composed of approximately 100 billion nerve cells—neurons—which have the capacity to input and output electrochemical pulses. These pulses, constantly switching on and off, act as signals to other neurons. Biologically, neurons are little different from other cells in the human body, except for their amazing ability to receive and transmit electrochemical messages.

A neuron is composed of three basic parts: a blob-like body, or *soma*; cable-like projections, called *axons*; and nerve endings, called dendrites. The axon carries electrochemical messages along the length of the neuron. At the end of each axon are the *synapses*, tiny branch-like projections.

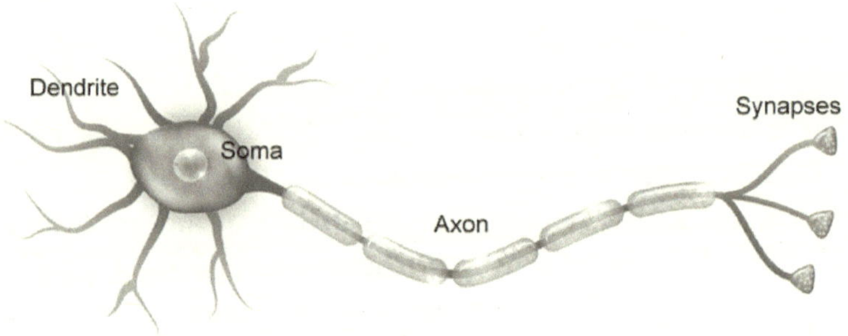

The dendrites form connections with other cells, enabling the neuron to communicate with other neurons and to perceive signals from the environment.

Neurons come in many sizes and shapes, depending on their functions. Motor neurons, which control muscle contractions, have a soma on one end, a long axon in the middle, and dendrites on the opposite end.

Sensory neurons, which perceive external stimuli, have dendrites on both ends, connected by a long axon with a soma in the middle. Some neurons fire off hundreds of electrochemical signals per second.

The researcher's challenge is to figure out how all this wiring works—how information is processed through those connections and which neurons are used in the process. For decades, neuroscientists believed human memories are stored in the synapses at the end of the cable-like axon. However, recent research indicates that memories are stored inside brain cells and can actually be refreshed by electrical stimulation, upending virtually every previous scientific assumption about human memory.

The average human brain can perform about 10 million billion operations per second, using only about 10 to 25 watts of electricity. For perspective, the most powerful supercomputer ever built would require 10 million times more power than that to do the same amount of work.

Neurologists have successfully mapped virtually the entirety of what we think of as "ourselves" using electrical stimulation of specific locations in the brain. Electrical impulses can make us happy or sad, euphoric or depressed, sexually aroused or antagonistic, benevolent or belligerent, make us love or hate; they can delete or alter memories, make us hunger or feel satiated, or change our personalities.

The sum of all our being, our consciousness, emotions, memories, ideas, and cognition, resides in the brain in the form of complex electrochemical codes.

Connectomes and ANNs

The U.S. government's Brain Activity Map (BAM) project was established to fund research to determine exactly how the brain generates thoughts, stores memories, and achieves consciousness. The aim is to develop a technology that will allow scientists to follow a thought process by recording every blip of every one of the thousands, and possibly millions, of neurons involved. According to George Church, a biologist at Harvard University, "We don't just want to see the wires, but also the messages going over the wires."

The Human Connectome Project (HCP) was launched by the National Institutes of Health in 2009 to build a circuit diagram of the anatomical and functional connectivity of the human brain. The hope was to produce a body of data to facilitate research into brain disorders such as dyslexia, autism, Alzheimer's disease, and schizophrenia. The production and study of such maps, or connectomes, became known as connectomics. The term "connectome" was first used in 2005, by Olaf Sporns at Indiana University and Dr. Patrick Hagmann at Lausanne University Hospital, referring to a map of the neural connections within the brain. In their 2005 paper, "The Human Connectome," they wrote:

> *"The connectome will significantly increase our understanding of how functional brain states emerge from their underlying structural substrate, and will provide new mechanistic insights into how brain function is affected if this structural substrate is disrupted."*

Based on the principles of connectomics, scientists have succeeding in constructing an accurate network map of a mouse's retina and primary visual cortex.

However, the general goal of biological intelligence research is even more ambitious: to develop an understanding of intelligent systems, by studying how a neural-based system becomes capable of intelligent behavior. Such research focuses on a broad spectrum of disciplines, from biochemical, molecular, and cellular studies to connectomes, computational neuroscience, and cognitive science.

The ultimate goal is to understand how the human brain processes sensory information and represents knowledge, and to use this knowledge to implement such processes in the design of intelligent devices.

An intelligent system, whether biological or electronic, must be capable of performing four basic activities. First, it must be able to perceive its environment. Second, it must have memory in which to store its perceptions. Third, it must be capable of applying its perceptions to formulate behavior and evaluate the effectiveness of its actions. Fourth, it must be able to autonomously communicate with other intelligent systems.

One approach to the challenge is the development of artificial neural networks (ANNs). Such networks are modeled loosely after biological neural networks, particularly the human brain. Like an human's nervous system, an ANN is a system of interconnected "neurons" that communicate with one another via encoded electronic messages, using statistics to "train" the network based on experience.

Whereas ANNs are useful for simple machine learning tasks, such as static image recognition and some types of pattern recognition, they are limited in their ability to model time and feedback. From a resource standpoint, ANNs are woefully inefficient, requiring enormous numbers of servers to accomplish such tasks as image recognition and language translation.

Because of these inherent limitations, ANNs are unlikely to ever approach artificial general intelligence.

In truth, Deep Learning (DL) networks are only metaphorically similar to the neural networks in biological brains.

A typical biological neuron has several hundreds of proximal synapses, representing only about ten percent of all the synapses on a nerve cell. A simulated neuron in an ANN has a few dozen synapses. The proximal synapses on a biological neuron recognize dozens of unique patterns, while those of a simulated neuron fixate on one pattern at a time.

Hierarchical Temporary Memory (HTM) networks are modeled after some of the structural and algorithmic properties of a human brain's neocortex.

A typical HTM network is a tree-shaped hierarchy of various levels composed of smaller elements called nodes or columns. The network "learns" to recognize images by analyzing a sequence of spatial patterns input to its nodes. The learning process consists of two stages:

During a process called **spatial pooling**, frequently observed patterns are memorized. Patterns that are significantly similar to each other are treated as the same instance, or "coincidence." Numerous input patterns are reduced to a manageable number of known coincidences.

During a process called **temporal pooling**, coincidences that have a high probability of following each other are grouped together based on their sequence over time. Each group of patterns is referred to as a "cause."

Inference takes place when an HTM node calculates the probabilities that a pattern belongs to each known coincidence and temporal group. The set of probabilities assigned to these groups represents the node's "belief" about the input pattern.

All computers store information in “dense” representations such as a 32-bit word in which any bit may have a value of either 1 or 0. However, of a human neocortex's 100 billion neurons, only a small percentage are active at any given time.

This phenomenon is referred to as sparse distributed representation, or SDR.

An HTM network also uses SDRs. For example, a typical HTM might have 64,000 artificial neurons, only 40 of which might be active at once. Neither a human brain nor an HTM network could process information otherwise.

A dense representation is based on a small number of switches, with a set value assigned to all the switches at the same time. For example, a text character is represented by a computer as eight switches, or bits. Each combination of bits has a specific value assigned to it. Such dense representations are useful for storing large amounts of data, but they are not comparable to SDRs. In a dense representation, switching a single bit results in a completely different value, with no shared meaning in relation to other represented information.

The neurons in a human's brain learn to respond to numerous unique patterns. Temporal pooling is an absolute requirement for inference to occur. For a cell to recognize all these patterns transmitted on its proximal dendrites requires that the patterns to be recognized are sparse. This process can only be understood in the context of SDRs.

An even more ambitious project has been launched by a consortium of universities and IBM computer labs, to put the computing power of a human brain on a silicon chip no larger than two liters in volume. The program, SyNAPSE, is funded by DARPA.

The goal is to build a microprocessor with 10 billion artificial "neurons" and 100 trillion "synapses," effectively replicating one hemisphere of a human brain. The project, if successful, will result from a culmination of thirty years of research on simulated neural networks. Called "neuromorphic processing," the computing activities performed by the neural processors could solve problems too complex for conventional computers.

According to SyNAPSE 's team leader, Dharmendra Modha, such neuromorphic processing will not replace conventional computing, but enhance it—for example, through advanced pattern recognition, such as the ability to identify a single face in a crowd. In fact, the neural microprocessor would be much less efficient at math than a conventional processor.

Just as a conventional computer lacks a suitable architecture to reproduce a brain, a neuroprocessor would be incapable of adding, subtracting, multiplying, and dividing at the incredible speed of which conventional computers are capable.

Memcomputers

A different approach at simulating the brain has been undertaken by theoretical physicists at the University of California at San Diego. Their design calls for components that are capable of acting as both processors and memory banks. In conventional computers, processors can execute programming instructions but cannot store memory, whereas memory chips cannot do processing. The new dual-duty components would replace conventional circuit parts such as transistors, capacitors, and inductors with memristors, memcapacitors, and meminductors. Such components, already available in experimental form, could become the basis for a machine capable of unmatched processing speed—the memcomputer. Calculations that would take a conventional computer decades to complete would take mere seconds for a memcomputer to solve. Instead of transferring data back and forth between processors and memory, a memcomputer's components would be able to solve problems on the spot and store the solutions.

The concept of memristors actually originated in the 1970s, at the University of California at Berkeley, but remained theoretical until 2008, when Hewlett-Packard succeeded in developing memory elements that could shift resistance, like a conventional circuit resister, or maintain its current state, like a memory cell.

At present, memcomputers exist only as simulations, but the technology to fabricate the components already exists. The initial obstacle will be software capable of taking advantage of the gargantuan processing power made available by the new architecture. Literally, it could take decades to create a software program to enable the memcomputer to solve within seconds a complex problem that would take decades for a conventional computer to solve.

An Artificial Synapse

In 2017, a team of researchers from Stanford University and Sandia National Laboratories produced an artificial synapse capable of mimicking how a real brain's synapses learn from the electrochemical signals receive. Modeled after a battery, the artificial synapse consists of three terminals spaced across two flexible films connected by an a saline solution, serving as an electrolyte. The synapse functions in a similar manner as a transistor, with one terminal controlling the flow of electrical current between the other two terminals.

It needs to be emphasized that all these emerging technologies, as promising as they may be, are as yet in their early infancy. What is prominently lacking is the "brainware"—the rich, incredibly complex program of electrochemical signals that constitute not just recognition and learning, but also experiencing, imagining, and creating.

As philosopher Steven Pinker opined in his book *The Language Instinct*, "the main lesson of thirty-five years of AI research is that the hard problems are easy and the easy problems are hard. The mental abilities of a four-year-old that we take for granted—recognizing a face, lifting a pencil, walking across a room, answering a question—in fact solve some of the hardest engineering problems ever conceived."

13

OLD MODELS MUST BE DISCARDED

The Not So Singular Singularity

"What we wish, we readily believe, and what we ourselves think, we imagine others think also."
Julius Caesar

The most enthusiastic advocates—as well as the most worried skeptics—of Artificial Intelligence envision a future when computer technology will have advanced so far that supercomputers will "wake up" as sentient beings, with all the mental capabilities as humans, but vastly superior in intelligence. Others cheer on the development of sophisticated mechanical brains into which humans will be able to upload their own minds, enabling their conscious selves to live forever—or at least as long as the mechanical brains still function.

The premise for these cyber dreams is "recursive self-improvement"—the notion that at some point computers will be capable of creating their own updates and enhancements, enabling them to design even more advanced computers. Eventually, the more advanced computers would spawn even brainier machines, and so on, eventuating in the creation of an exact neural replica of the human brain.

In both scenarios, machine intelligence continues to increase for all time, after crossing an event horizon where the intellects of the machines exceed our own. The pop science term for this imagined phenomenon is the Singularity. The term has roots in both mathematics and theoretical physics.

A mathematical singularity is a point at which the results of an equation are no longer predictable, or, in geometry, a point where all parallel lines meet. In physics, a singularity is a point in space and time in which matter becomes infinitely dense, primarily associated with Stephen Hawking's description of Black Holes.

Borrowing from Vigne, pop-science writer Ray Kurzweil, regarded by some as the "godfather" of the Singularity fad, defined the Singularity as

> *"... a future period during which the pace of technological change will be so rapid, its impact so deep, that human life will be irreversibly transformed."*

According to Kevin Kelly, the founder *of Wired Magazine*, the Singularity is the point at which "all the change in the last million years will be superseded by the change in the next five minutes."

James Martin, a leader of the Visionary Futurist movement, predicts the Singularity will occur as "a break in human evolution that will be caused by the staggering speed of technological evolution."

In one version of AI Singularity, humans and machines will merge as one, replacing humanity with a new breed of human-machine entities. In another version, humans and computers will compete for existence, with *Homo Sapiens* as the ultimate loser. Various hybrids of this latter version range from total machine domination to the total extinction of humankind. The conclusion of all these not-so-singular Singularity theories is a new phase of human existence, transformed forever by the rise of superintelligent machines.

Though AI is already transforming human lives and livelihoods at an astonishing pace, the Singularity theory is far from a certainty.

Singularity Origins

As described in Chapter 2, the so-called Singularity, as it pertains to machine intelligence, is attributed to a science fiction writer, Vernor Vinge. In a speech to a NASA-sponsored gathering of technology workers, he speculated: "There may be developed computers that are 'awake' and superhumanly intelligent." Further to this development, "large computer networks (and their associated users) may wake up as a superhumanly intelligent entity." He went on to dub such an event "the Singularity," defining it as

> *"...a point where our old models must be discarded and a new reality rules."*

Vigne attributes the use of the term Singularity in the context of technological advancement to a quote by an acquaintance of John von Neumann, in 1953:

> *"One conversation centered on the ever accelerating progress of technology and changes in the mode of human life, which gives the appearance of approaching some essential singularity in the*

> *history of the race beyond which human affairs, as we know them, could not continue."*

In his speech, Vigne acknowledged that Von Neumann was apparently "thinking of normal progress, not the creation of superhuman intellect." Nevertheless, Vigne was certain that "the end of the human era" would occur as early as 2005 but no later than 2030.

Ray Kurzweil, in his speculative book *The Singularity is Near,* predicted that computers will become sensient beings by 2029 and that, by 2045, thinking machines will be "billions of times more powerful than unaided human intelligence." As described in Chapter 2, Nick Bostrom, a philosophy professor at Oxford University, mused that a post-Singularity supercomputer programmed to manufacture paper clips might destroy humanity in order to convert our atoms into paper clips.

According to the movement's enthusiasts, the Singularity will arrive through momentum. Supercomputers will design, engineer, and build gènius computers. The resulting machine-human super species will form collaborative hive minds. At that point, human existence will be redefined.

"The physical extinction of the human race is one possibility," Vinge speculated, though another possibility is a future ruled by "benevolent gods." Whatever the outcome, the world as we know it will have ended.

Some proponents believe in a utopian Singularity, with machine-enhanced humans transcending their biological limitations. Others foresee humans relinquishing most of their abilities and becoming absorbed into AI-based organisms composed of both biological and mechanical components.

As noted in Chapter 11, most of the pop science speculation about the Singularity has been espoused by math or philosophy teachers, science fiction writers, diet fad advocates, entrepreneurs, and corporate spokespeople. Computer scientists actively involved in AI research, development, and deployment tend not to be obsessed with the rise of robots intent on the extinction of humankind.

Science and the Singularity

From the standpoint of both technology and resources, as of this writing we are nowhere near being able to develop sensient machines, or, for that matter, "self-recursive" machines capable of designing, building, and programming sensient machines. Despite being able to defeat world champion chess players and *Jeopardy* contestants, even the most superintelligent computers lag light-years behind an ordinary human child in terms of language acquisition, intuition, common sense, and interaction with the physical world.

A five-year-old girl viewing a piano fall from a tenth-story window directly above her instantly recognizes and responds to the peril by leaping out of harm's way. In contrast, a computer would first have to search millions of images and video files, construct and perform a complicated motion simulation, know the exact size and weight of the piano, analyze the tactile qualities of the sidewalk, and take into consideration its own ability to resist being crushed into a pile of rubble, among numerous other factors.

However, if, like the U.S. Army's robot land mine, the computer happens to be equipped with legs, it might in fact leap out of harm's way and, if empowered by deep learning software, preserve the moment for the future. No matter what the outcome, unlike the child, neither the computer nor the land mine will experience fear, emotion, or happiness—

essential components of every human experience and decision. Of course, for some proponents of the human-machine Singularity, this might be a good thing.

Singularity enthusiasts have been predicting that the event horizon is near for several decades. The "near future" in these forecasts is a forever-moving target. As Stuart Armstrong, a research fellow at Oxford University, once remarked, "AI predictions are very hard to get right. Timeline predictions are particularly worthless."

As an example, in 1950, Alan Turing predicted that a computer would be able to pass his namesake Test—thereby supposedly proving itself a sensient being—by the year 2000. While AI has made dramatic progress, for most AI researchers, the realization of conscious computers is still an extremely distant prospect. In the opinion of Yann LeCun, professor of computer and neural science at New York University, "in terms of computational ability, even the most powerful computers in the world are just approaching that of an insect."

In an article, "The Singularity Isn't Near," Paul Allen and Mark Greaves debunked the often-cited though empirically groundless "Moore's Law":

> *"If the singularity is to arrive by 2045, it will take unforeseeable and fundamentally unpredictable breakthroughs, and not because the Law of Accelerating Returns made it the inevitable result of a specific exponential rate of progress."*

Thomas Hartsfield noted:

"It seems that AI is always predicted, by most experts, to be something like 15 to 25 years away from the present."

To quote Robin Hanson, chief scientist at Consensus Point, some AI researchers believe that "without any acceleration it might take between 200 and 400 years to achieve the goal," and some would argue that progress towards achieving such a goal is actually decelerating.

In reality, we are already in the midst of a technological Singularity. Machines already perform many intelligent tasks formerly relegated to humans. Since the invention of the printing press, humans have continuously redefined intelligence and transferred those tasks to machines.

The cold truth is that unlimited development and self-recursion of intelligent machines is resource-intensive. Besides the enormous financial resources required, scarce human resources are required in the form of humans of superior intelligence capable of designing, engineering, and programming the first generation of self-recursive machines. Superior intellects at any given time in human history are limited in supply. It's worth noting that, historically, humans with the most brilliant minds have often chosen to devote their cognitive powers to philosophy and the arts, rather than applied sciences.

In short, even if the technology is possible, the financial and intellectual resources may not be available to make the Singularity dream a reality. Furthermore, it cannot be dismissed that computers are not really analogous to human brains. Computer brains do not, in fact, function in precisely the same way as our own. Neural networks are not composed of neurons; in fact, computer "neurons" do not behave at all like the neurons in a brain. While good at fuzzy logic and distinguishing images, speech, and the flow of pedestrians through shopping malls, neural networks are not even vaguely analogous to human brain matter.

Despite the intrigue and, for some, the excitement, associated with the idea of uploading a human mind into a computer, few scientists working in the AI field are focused on the Singularity movement or its dreams of machines emerging from sleep as sensient beings.

The idea that a technology, existing or conceivable, is capable of storing the rich tapestry of a human memory or the innate linguistic functions with which humans are born, is theoretical at best. The notion that non-self-recursive humans are capable of developing self-recursive machines that will "wake up" as sensient beings is still hypothetical.

No breakthrough in neuroscience to date has established that a mind is analogous to computer software, or that a brain functions similarly to computer hardware. Based on our current knowledge, human minds are dependent on the gray matter of the brain, or "wetware." As of yet, there is no mechanical equivalent of that wetware, nor any feasible method of creating it.

Lacking a scientific basis, Vigne's and Kurzweil's Singularity, sensationalized in pop-science books, articles, blogs, and conference agendas, could well remain mostly a belief system, if not a fad. Conceivably, in the distant future, the Singularity dream of a human-machine super species could seem as naive to historians as people in Victorian times getting dressed up to make phone calls.

The Scientific Solution

A possible solution to the wetware challenge is to "grow" brain tissue in the lab from a human brain. Scientists at the

Institute of Molecular Biotechnology (IMBA) of the Austrian Academy of Sciences (OeAW), led by Dr. Jürgen Knoblich have developed complex human brain tissue made from stem cells in a laboratory. These mini brains, only a few millimeters in size, developed several discrete but interdependent brain regions, including a cerebral cortex.

Knoblich's team extracted tissue fragments from a layer of cells in the brain, from which the nervous system originates. These fragments were embedded in a gel, providing a foundation for complex tissue growth. To enhance the absorption of nutrients, the culture was placed in spinning bioreactor. Within weeks, defined brain regions were formed, including a cerebral cortex, retina, meninges, and a choroid plexus. The brain-like blobs reached a maximum size after two months in the spinning bioreactor.

Dr. Madeline A. Lancaster, a member of the research team, projects that "in addition to the potential for new insights into the development of human brain disorders, mini brains will also be of great interest to the pharmaceutical and chemical industries." The Austrian experiment demonstrated that cultivating fully functional wetware may be possible. However, whether it would be possible to transfer consciousness from a living brain to test tube-grown wet matter remains, at this stage, speculation.

A more likely integration of human and machine will occur not by uploading the mind into a machine, but through bioenhancement—augmenting the brain and body with microchip implants, bioengineered organs, and cybernetic limbs. Bioengineering is nearing the point where substituting organs with lab-grown replacements will become standard procedure. Transplanted organs will be manufactured using stem cells from a patient's own body, from bone marrow, brain tissue, or any number of sources. Replacing hearts, livers, lungs, kidneys, and other organs will increase life expectancy dramatically.

Microchip brain implants (as described in Chapter 9) have already been used to restore lost memory. The ability to replace aging or faulty parts of the brain will reverse aging and extend mental agility as long as the brain can be kept alive.

A human brain is dependent on its body as much as the body is dependent on its brain. It has been demonstrated that a human can control robotic devices, such as hands, legs, and wheelchairs. Several technologies allow patients to control computers, prosthetics, and other devices using signals captured from nerves, muscles, or the brain, using Electro-encephalography (EEG).

A robotic wheelchair developed by researchers at the Federal Institute of Technology in Lausanne, Switzerland, uses AI programming that can take a simple command like "go left" and perform the desired action while navigating around objects. A patient controls the wheelchair simply by imagining the movement of a part of the body. Thinking of moving the left hand tells the chair to turn left. Commands can also be triggered by performing mental tasks such as arithmetic.

As mind-machine interfaces are perfected, replacing aging body parts with cybernetic equivalents will become routine. Given sufficient resources, human longevity could be extended for hundreds of years by such augmentation and repair.

Unfortunately, there is no guarantee such resources will be available—except, possibly, for the very rich—or that an intervening event such as a pandemic, nuclear war, or solar storm will not take place.

The longer an organism endures, whether biological or cybernetic, the higher the odds that it will become extinct. In terms of infinity, the likelihood of extinction is one hundred percent.

14

IF YOU DIE BEFORE YOU WAKE

Transhumanism and the Quest for Machine Immortality

"We do not live in order to experience death."
Ludwig Wittgenstein

Stephen Hawking, at a screening of a film about his life, told the crowd, "I think the brain is like a program in the mind, which is like a computer, so it's theoretically possible to copy the brain onto a computer and so provide a form of life after death." He admitted, however, "this is way beyond our present capabilities." Undoubtedly, what he was trying to say was that "the mind is like a program in the brain, which is like a computer." Even that statement is based more on philosophical musing than scientific evidence.

The notion that a human mind is a type of programming analogous to computer software is tempting but naive. As the human genome project proved, the more we explore our biological qualities, the less we understand. Mapping the human genome did not, as some had predicted, result in the ability to clone fully grown people. Likewise, the development of computer hardware and software capable of mimicking the heuristic processes underlying human reasoning is far from analogous to transferring an intact mind from a brain to a computer.

Mind Transfer

The peculiar branch of the Singularity movement that enthusiastically embraces the notion of mind transfer is often referred to as "Transhumanism." Its theme is the achievement of immortality through mind transfer. Of course, as stated earlier in this book, immortality is a scientific impossibility; eventually, all matter—even atoms and quarks—will cease to exist. To quote Joseph Scalise, "The lights are going out, but nobody alive today, or even in the next hundred million years, will be around to see it happen."

Sometime between 200 billion and 3.3 trillion years from now, the physical universe will die. The earth will have disintegrated long before, as soon as 100 million years from now.

In this regard, the ultimate goal of Transhumanism is more realistically viewed as "extremely extended longevity"—i.e., as long as the machines that house the transferred minds, and the power source that supplies them, continue to exist. This glamorous concept is tantalizing enough, at least superficially, that it bears exploring.

In Ray Kurzweil's opinion, mind transfer will be possible by the year 2055. According to him, "based on conservative estimates of the amount of computation you need to functionally simulate a human brain, we'll be able to expand the scope of our intelligence a billion-fold." Realistically, the pop-science writer's predictions regarding the rise of a robot super-race and the eventuality of mind transfer are based on broad generalities about technology, not specifics based on neuroscience or computer programming.

The premise of mind transfer requires the acceptance of five major assumptions (in addition to hundreds of more detailed considerations):

1. A mind is analogous to computer software.

2. A brain is analogous to computer hardware.

3. Intact human memories can be stored electronically in the same way that data is stored by a computer.

4. If a human brain is replicated mechanically and electronically in exact or approximate detail, human consciousness will result, or at least be possible.

5. Human minds do not depend on a specific biological medium or process that cannot be reproduced electronically.

Unless all these assumptions are demonstrably true, the process is intrinsically impossible. Predictions and philosophy aside, the feasibility depends on viable procedures for analyzing and duplicating a specific brain, decoding and uploading the mind to the machine, and verifying that the transfer is successful. The issues and obstacles are obvious. To date, several different techniques have been described.

One theoretical procedure involves creating an "empty" artificial brain—a computer that already has all the capabilities of a human brain. The mind of the human subject would be extracted—for example, by means of electrodes attached to synapses throughout the subject's brain—and then decoded by a superintelligent computer, which would transfer the signals to the waiting artificial brain. This method would require knowing exactly how every cell in a specific human brain functions, down to the most microscopic detail. Billions of electrodes would be required simply to "read" the information imparted by the brain's electrochemical activity.

A second technique involves scanning the subject's brain and copying its structure precisely. The scanning and copying might take place simultaneously, or at different times. With this method, copying the brain's structure is more important than understanding how it works.

In a variation of this proposal, a superintelligent robot surgeon would remove and scan tiny portions of the subject's brain, and then create software that would precisely model the behavior of the scanned tissue. The robot surgeon would then install the mind-duplicating software on a computer and verify its performance to that of the original brain tissue.

In this scenario, the human subject would be awake during the procedure, so that he or she would be able to interact with the computer simulation as it is constructed. Once the subject is satisfied that the simulation is perfect, the connection would be secured, and the original brain tissue removed. When the robot has processed the subject's entire brain, the transfer would be complete.

At this point, the subject's brain will have been completely dissected and removed from the skull, with his or her mind now residing in the circuitry of the computer in the form of a software program reconstructed by the robot surgeon.

One potential obstacle to this approach that proponents may have failed to consider is that the procedure would only capture the existing state of the brain at the time of the transfer—in fact, only the state of each scanned portion. Such a procedure would take quite a long time to complete, so the brain—and more particularly the mind—would be in different states as the simulation is assembled.

For example, perceptual information is stored by the brain in a region called the *hippocampus*, in a temporary memory pool. Days or weeks later, the information is moved to the cerebral cortex for long-term storage. Not all information even makes the trip and is permanently lost. From the cortex, the memories may later be moved to the synapses—the tendril-like branches at the tip of the neurons—from where they can be recalled more readily. The scan-and-model procedure, assuming it worked at all, could scramble the subject's long- and short-term memory or create a permanent hallucinogenic state.

The biggest obstacle may be the fact that a brain's structure is not a static set of neurons and synapses. Synaptic relays are developed within the brain as perceptions are acquired, emotions are experienced, and memories are formed. In other words, the neural network for any given brain is constructed from birth for that person's mind—and none other.

It bears repeating that the mind transfer process would take a very long time. To dissect, model, scan, program, and test an entire brain using the fastest computer technology available today would take millions of years. Ostensibly, according to pop science predictions, post-Singularity super-computers will perform at speeds billions of times faster. However, since the process involves the human subject verifying each piece of the simulation portion by portion, the critical path will forever remain based on human time, not machine time. It's not likely that the entire process could be completed before the subject dies, even under artificial life support.

A similar but less invasive approach would be to use implanted electrodes to analyze and image the brain's 1,000 trillion neurons and synapses. If—and only if—the electric impulses are analogous to computer software, in theory they might be able to be decoded by a superintelligent computer and copied to a host artificial brain in a machine-readable format.

This method would require a detailed map of exactly which, when, how, and for what purpose all the neurons in the subject's brain are communicating with one another at any given time. Should this approach prove successful, the mind theoretically should then be schizophrenic, with two separate, parallel identities. The biological human's mental capacities would inexorably deteriorate with age, while the computer-housed mind would remain in exactly the same state as when it was uploaded.

Obstacles and Challenges

The standard Transhumanist answer to any potential obstacles or obvious impossibilities is that "the self-recursive superintelligent computers will have solved the problem by then." For example, for any mind transfer scenario to work, it must be assumed that supercomputers will have discovered and recorded all there is to know about a human brain's neural structure, function, and growth.

Any discussion of mind transfer must consider that a mandatory component of brain activity is sleep and, with it, dreaming. Sleep is required by the body for regeneration. A human indefinitely deprived of sleep would die.

In a biological brain, nerve-signaling chemicals called neurotransmitters control whether we are asleep or awake, by acting on different groups of neurons. A chemical called Adenosine builds up in our blood while we are awake and causes drowsiness, signaling neurons at the base of the brain to switch off the neurotransmitters that keep us awake.

REM (rapid eye movement) sleep—which occurs just after deep sleep—begins with signals from an area at the base of the brain called the pons. These signals travel to a different region called the thalamus, which relays them to the cerebral cortex, the outer layer of the brain responsible for learning, thinking, and organizing information. The pons also sends signals that shut off neurons in the spinal cord, causing temporary paralysis of the limb muscles. If something interferes with this paralysis, people will begin to physically "act out" their dreams—a dangerous problem called REM sleep behavior disorder.

REM sleep stimulates the brain regions used in learning. This may be important for normal brain development during infancy, which would explain why infants spend much more time in REM sleep than adults.

Dreams are the cortex's attempt to find meaning in the random signals that it receives during REM sleep. The cortex is the part of the brain that interprets and organizes information from the environment during consciousness. Receiving random signals from the pons during REM sleep, the cortex, as it tries to interpret these signals, creates a story out of fragmented brain activity.

In an artificial brain, neurotransmitters and their effects would have to be simulated. Since the construct would have neither blood nor hormones, these biological necessities would have to be simulated, also. In theory, a transferred mind would have no need to sleep and would never experience drowsiness. Regeneration of neurons, which occurs during sleep, would not be required, either. However, the consequence of perpetual sleeplessness on the regions of the brain used in learning could result in deterioration of the transferred mind's ability to assimilate, organize, and recall experiences.

Dreams are described by neurologists as random electronic noise, though undoubtedly they create both short and long term memories. Everyone routinely forgets dream details shortly after wakening, but some details linger, often for years, as memories of recurring people, places, events, objects, and environments. Some dreams are so vivid that they seem indistinguishable from reality. Yet not all dreaming consists of random noise.

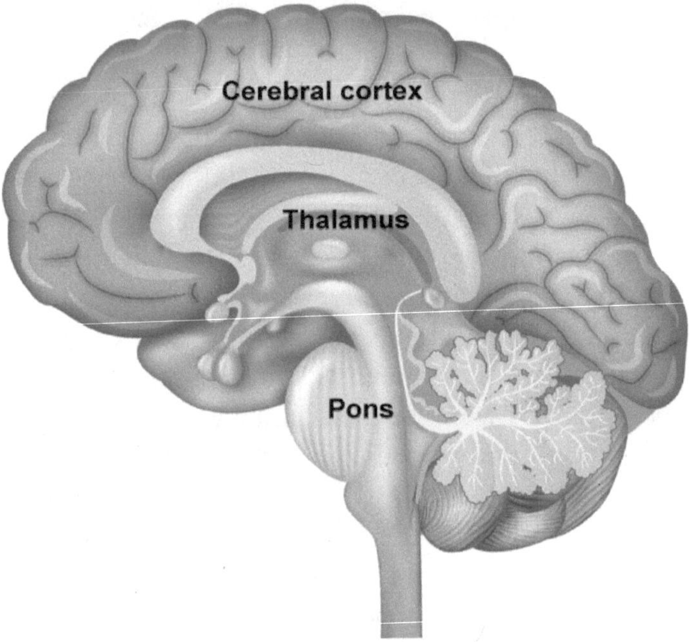

I have actually solved numerous computer programming problems in dreams—evidence that cognition is active even during sleep. Many people report waking in the middle of the night to write down ideas that came to them in dreams. Nevertheless, most dreams occur not as software code or wish lists, but as imagined experiences, often with realistic plots and characterization, though just as often nonsensical.

Would minds housed in computers or robots dream? Since sleep is a biological necessity that would be ignored by the transfer of a mind to a computer, technically there would be no need or mechanism for dreaming. Yet memories retained from past dreams of a former biological self would continue to reside in the machine self. As a result, the machine mind would, at a minimum, have a false perception of reality and could very well live in a permanent state of hallucination or psychosis—a phenomenon the mind transfer technologists might not even be able to detect.

If the function of every region in the brain is duplicated exactly, sleep and dreaming still might be induced, though the "chemical release" would be simulated.

First and foremost, mind transfer or "consciousness uploading" is based on the premise that organic minds are no different than digital computers. However, not everyone involved in neuroscience and AI research is convinced that the brain-computer analogy is valid. There is an ongoing debate among neuroscientists, computer scientists, and philosophy professors, as to whether it is even possible to reverse-engineer or duplicate a human brain electronically.

To quote science writer George Dvorksy, "the computational theory of mind, in essence, says that your brain works like a computer...it takes input from the outside world, then performs algorithms to produce output in the form of mental state or action. In other words, it claims that the brain is an information processor where your mind is 'software' that runs on the 'hardware' of the brain."

Another science writer, Alex Knapp, argues that a human mind "is best understood, not as software, but rather as an emergent property of the physical brain." Consequently, "building an artificial intelligence with the same level of complexity as that of a human intelligence isn't a matter of just finding the right algorithms and putting it together." Knapp observes that "the end result of a non-human, sapient intelligence would be very alien to our understanding, possibly to the point of noncomprehension. Electric circuits simply function differently than electrochemical ones, and so it's likely that any sapient properties would emerge quite differently."

Brazilian neuroscientist Miguel Nicolelis is more emphatic that "the brain is not computable and no engineering can reproduce it." Nicolelis argues that human consciousness will never be replicated mechanically because it results from unpredictable, nonlinear interactions among billions of cells.

David Chalmers is Director of the Centre for Consciousness at the Australian National University and also Professor of Philosophy at New York University. In his essay "Facing Up to the Problem of Consciousness," published in the Journal of Consciousness Studies, he wondered:

> *"How can we explain why there is something it is like to entertain a mental image, or to experience an emotion? It is widely agreed that experience arises from a physical basis, but we have no good explanation of why and how it so arises. Why should physical processing give rise to a rich inner life at all? It seems objectively unreasonable that it should, and yet it does."*

He offered that "consciousness poses the most baffling problems in the science of the mind. There is nothing that we know more intimately than conscious experience, but there is nothing that is harder to explain."

Chalmers observed that awareness and conscious experience should be classified as two different phenomena. Awareness, which consists of easily defined neural processes, involves the ability discriminate, categorize, and react to environmental stimuli; focus attention; and deliberately control behavior. Conscious experience, which varies from one person to another, is subjective. Some people prefer the color red to blue, whereas others delight in opera as opposed to rock and roll. Such subjective perceptions are capable of modifying or tainting the experience stored by the brain.

According to Chalmers, "to account for conscious experience, we need an extra ingredient in the explanation." What exactly that ingredient might be—and why it should account for conscious experience—is the "hard" problem.

> *"There is no shortage of extra ingredients to be had. Some propose an injection of chaos and nonlinear dynamics. Some think that the key lies in non-algorithmic processing. Some appeal to future discoveries in neurophysiology. Some suppose that the key to the mystery will lie at the level of quantum mechanics. It is easy to see why all these suggestions are put forward. None of the old methods work, so the solution must lie with something new."*

Indeed, the relationship between consciousness and intentional mental states, such as belief, thought, and comprehension, is not yet understood. "The moral of all this," Chalmers espoused, "is that you can't explain conscious experience on the cheap."

Scientists so far have no good explanation for why we even have consciousness, other than its positive adaptive value to this point in our evolution.

Besides cognition, the brain is also responsible for regulating the body's organs, which, with a body no longer present, would have to be simulated by the artificial brain's software. The regulation and release of hormones responsible for such phenomena as emotions, growth, sex drive, heart rate, and so forth, would also have to be simulated. The effects, since there would be no physical body to regulate, would exist only in simulation—e.g., in a virtual reality program. When the artificial "pituitary gland" releases simulated "growth hormone," the machine, of course, would not actually grow, but a simulation of growth would be required to keep the "gland" functioning normally.

The same principle would apply to simulated hormones that increase sex drive, anger, and aggressiveness, with unpredictable effects on the computer-housed mind. If the implanted mind continues to function as it did in its former biological body, eventual irreversible mental derangement can't be ruled out.

Because every transplanted mind would be based on a unique brain architecture, not only its capabilities, predilections, biases, and *a priori* knowledge, but also its deficiencies, would be transferred to the artificial brain.

One sect of the Transhumanism cult envisions that transplanted minds will be augmented with new and amazing powers—for example, faster processing speed on par with a superintelligent computer, or connectivity to a vast network containing the sum total of all human knowledge. This premise assumes, of course, that the mind doesn't depend on the specific circuit rate of its biological brain, and that it is capable of absorbing, storing, and comprehending the entirety of human knowledge in digital form.

These questions will remain unanswered until mind-to-computer transfers are actually attempted.

The ultimate fate of mind transfer technology hinges on the theory that duplicating the physical architecture of the human brain with electronic circuitry will automatically enable a machine to host a mind. To translate the theory into fact, human test subjects will have to put their brains, lives, and minds on the line. Just as pioneers and astronauts risked their lives in exploration, mind transfer volunteers will have to sacrifice everything in their devotion to the theory. Many attempts to perfect mind transfer technology may be required, resulting in scores—or possibly hundreds—of deaths, with the volunteers essentially serving as laboratory animals. It may not even be possible to credibly verify that a transfer is successful. The eventuality of a transferred mind ending up as no more than electronic "noise" can't be discounted.

Hosting a Mind

Cognition is relatively easy to mimic—for example, how we analyze information, recall a memory, make judgments, and solve problems. A more difficult challenge is to determine how sensations are translated into subjective feelings, how and why mental images are formed, or the process by which emotions are experienced.

Noam Chomsky postulated that human language is an extension of an inborn capacity within every human infant for mental imaging and thought creation, which he termed "Mentalese." This capacity precedes the development of our minds and is deeply ingrained in our infant brains. Mind transfer methods fail to account for either the mandatory host qualities of biological wetware or the underlying Mentalese required to create thought. While cognitive functions may be simulated on a neuronal level, no technology has been envisioned that would be capable of decoding and recording the processes of thought creation, emotion, or rich memory.

Nevertheless, Transhumanism has risen to the level of a religious belief system among technocult worshippers longing for immortality in a box. Uploading a mind to a computer is referred to as "crossing to the other side," a phrase popular with drug users for entering a state of altered consciousness. To believers, skeptics are "deathers."

Whether fanciful or feasible, the notion of mind transfer is for some people an incredibly tantalizing and ambitious goal. Though outliving the universe is a physical impossibility, what would you give for, say, an extra 100,000 years or so—though not in a human body, but electronically simulated on a microchip?

Let's just say, you'll have ample time on your hands (if only you had hands), to contemplate Hamlet's soliliquy: "to sleep, perchance to dream."

15

THE WORLD WE TAKE FOR GRANTED

The Vulnerability of the Machine

"The past is always tense, the future perfect."
Zadie Smith

Voltaire said, "Everything is fine today: That is our illusion." Indeed, a prerequisite to the continued advancement of AI is the perpetuation of the premise, or some might say, the illusion, that "everything is fine today." To embrace the ideal of self-recursive computers that one day will result in a superintelligent race of machines, it must be recognized that arriving at that point will be considerably more challenging than merely imagining or wishing it. In the cozy confines of the classroom, laboratory, or office cubicle, it is easy to overlook the fact that in the world outside everything indeed may not be "fine" enough.

Acknowledging the possibility that we humans by ourselves are incapable of solving and managing the many threats to their existence from global climate change, overpopulation, famine, disease, and war, artificial intelligence may hold the best promise of human survival. However, to quote Shoshana

Zuboff, Professor of Business Administration at Harvard Business School, "awareness requires a rupture with the world we take for granted."

External Influences

As mentioned in Chapter 13, finite human and financial resources are the fundamental delimiters of technological advancement, but so are external influences ranging from natural disasters to the volatility of infrastructures. Dwindling global resources and shrinking sustainability threaten to derail not only civilization, but also the quest to develop sensient machines. Ordinary planetary and astronomical influences are other serious perils to both existing and future integration of technology.

Modern civilization functions on the basis of elaborate technology-driven networks. Power grids, stock markets, international banking, air traffic control systems, transportation systems, and product distribution networks are examples. Increasing use and advancement of AI will arguably increase efficiency and profits, but also expose society to hitherto unimagined volatility.

In 2017, a system-wide failure of the British Airways computer system grounded hundreds of flights, stranding several thousands of passengers and incurring an estimated $1.2 billion in losses and damages.

Civilization would literally cease to function if the world's power grids failed. Quality of life for millions suffers during global financial crises. A global pandemic could spread within days via the airline network. Interruptions in the food distribution chain would leave grocery store shelves empty for weeks, even months. The more interconnected the world becomes, the greater the dependence on technology and the more dire the consequences of technological failure.

Contrary to the mantra repeatedly recited by worshippers of "Moore's Law," increasing multiplicity in the number of circuits on increasingly smaller chips will not, by itself, lead to the creation of a sensient computer. Enormous financial investment and human ingenuity will be required even to design, much less manufacture, autonomous self-recursive computers.

Unfortunately, computers thus far have proved to be very poor at writing software or updating their own design. A huge leap in development in both hardware and software is needed before machines begin designing and manufacturing newer, even more intelligent machines. Though the future is inevitable, the availability of funding and talent is determined by events, both human and natural.

Civilization in its current form possesses enormous financial, technological, cognitive, and manpower resources. Modern science is on the verge of developing effective solutions to the most formidable challenges facing humanity today—such as eradicating diseases, eliminating hunger and poverty, and solving ecological problems threatening the survival of life on this planet. Ironically, the critical issues that AI research aims to resolve could also lead to its downfall.

AI Winter and Spring

Since rule-based cognitive systems were first implemented in the 1960s, interest in AI—and consequently, funding for research—has waxed and waned over time, not unlike the length of women's skirts or men's sideburns. AI researchers have a term for periods of reduced interest and funding: *AI winter*. Two major AI winters occurred from 1974 to 1980, and from 1987 to 1993. In the early 1980s, a billion-dollar industry arose around AI expert systems, only to collapse in 1987. In the early 2000s, renewed interest in the possible applications of AI in medicine, industry, and warfare surfaced. By 2010, corporate investment in AI was at an all-time high, signaling an AI spring.

In 2014, Google, Inc. (now called Alphabet) purchased a small British company called DeepMind, devoted to "solving intelli-gence" by combining "machine learning and systems neuro-science to build powerful general-purpose learning algo-rithms." Google subsequently acquired more than a dozen other firms involved in AI and robotics. Other prominent corporate investments in AI research include the Facebook Artificial Intelligence Research lab ("FAIR"), Microsoft's Project Adam, and IBM's Watson.

Most of the hype surrounding AI today is conscientiously oriented to attract money—funding for research, capital investment, stock sales, or sales of products that either incorporate AI technology or are connected to the "Internet of Things." It's important to understand this fact when evaluating research papers, announcements of "breakthroughs," and "revolutionary" new products.

A second type of hype seeks to attract public interest and gain acceptance. At the government level, AI announcements seek to accomplish all three objectives: secure funding, get voters involved, and promote AI weapons as a public benefit, if not a national priority. A major challenge for AI developers in both the public and private sector will be to achieve true breakthroughs capable of being implemented as practical applications, before the next inevitable AI winter.

As of this writing, declining funding poses an imminent threat to the pace of scientific progress. Much of the public, as well as most government officials, do not have a general understanding of the scientific process or possess the awareness required to make critical decisions in an increasingly technological society. Industry is focused on applied research that will produce immediate commercial applications, but basic research is needed to create breakthroughs that provide the basis for applied research.

For example, in the area of medicine, creating treatments for many diseases will require new knowledge about basic cellular and molecular changes. Further advancements in cognitive computing will require an exhaustive and detailed understanding of the function and behavior of neurons.

Financial resources for overall scientific research have been declining dramatically over the past decade and appear poised for even more drastic reductions in the immediate future. Continued diminished funding will not only affect projects currently underway, but will also have a long-term impact on the number of people entering the field. Harvard University data show a clear shift toward corporate and foundation funding, away from government support. As a result, the impact of global economic health looms large. Even if a new era of regulation for the financial markets arises, it will not protect global economies from crises.

The price of an object bought, held, or sold for investment or profit experiences a predictable cycle of peaks and valleys. Real estate, securities, and rare metals are typical examples. Increasing demand causes the price to rise. As the object is repeatedly resold for gain, new purchasers join in, creating the illusion that there is no upward limit. At some point, a summit is reached where further price growth can no longer be sustained, due to extreme overvaluation.

This elementary economic phenomenon has resulted in financial crises throughout human history. As of this writing, investment in AI research and development at the corporate level is at an all time high. Predictably, the fortune of companies continues to be driven by an illusion that there will be no end to the scientific breakthroughs and stock market windfalls. The truth, however, is that interest and investment in AI will also reach its upward limit, dictated not by dreams of uploading minds into machines but by immutable economic realities. An "AI bubble burst" comparable to the infamous "dot com" and real estate crises that sent global economies into a downward spiral is, at some point, inevitable.

The Societal Collapse Obstacle

Pragmatically, even assuming that the necessary financial resources will be available, the hardware and software breakthroughs needed to create real progress toward the development of a self-aware computer may not come in time. A study of the "Use of Resources in the Collapse or Sustainability of Societies" by University of Maryland researchers Safa Motesharrei and Eugenia Kalnay, along with a team of natural and social scientists, warns of the possible collapse of civilization, as we know it, within 50 years. The research was sponsored by the NASA Goddard Space Flight Center. (NASA has since disavowed that it endorsed the study's findings.)

Analyzing five risk factors for societal collapse—population, climate, water, agriculture and energy—the researchers discovered that all such collapses over the past 5,000 years occurred when two phenomena occurred:

1. "Stretching of resources" due to the strain placed on the ecological carrying capacity.

2. Extreme unequal economic distribution between the rich ("Elites") and everyone else ("Commoners").

Prior to societal collapses, the "Elite" population restricts the flow of resources accessible to the "Commoners", in the process of accumulating a surplus of resources. This restriction, in turn, strains natural resources.

The eventual out-come is famine, followed by the breakdown of the society due to over-consumption of natural resources.

Technological advancements may temporarily spike the efficiency of resource consumption, but also raise both per-capita consumption and the scale of resource extraction. In time, the increased depletion of resources negates the benefits of increased efficiency.

In short, the impact of technology makes societal collapse even more likely.

Humans presently use more resources than the earth can replenish, and the planet's distribution of resources among the human population is massively unequal. Based on these facts, the report concludes that...

> *"closely reflecting the reality of the world today...*
> *we find that collapse is difficult to avoid."*

In another discomforting prediction, Stephen Hawking has forecast the end of humankind within a century. He believes the killer instinct and propensity for violence that enabled Homo Sapiens to survive prehistoric times will ultimately be our undoing.

With threats ranging from nuclear war and global warming to genetically engineered viruses, the iconic theoretical physicist finds it "difficult to imagine we'll still be around in 100 years."

The Hacker Obstacle

In truth, AI in its various current expressions is already vulnerable to a vast array of more immediate threats. The Internet of Things (IoT) is the latest pop-science fad, describing devices of all kinds connected to the internet, from

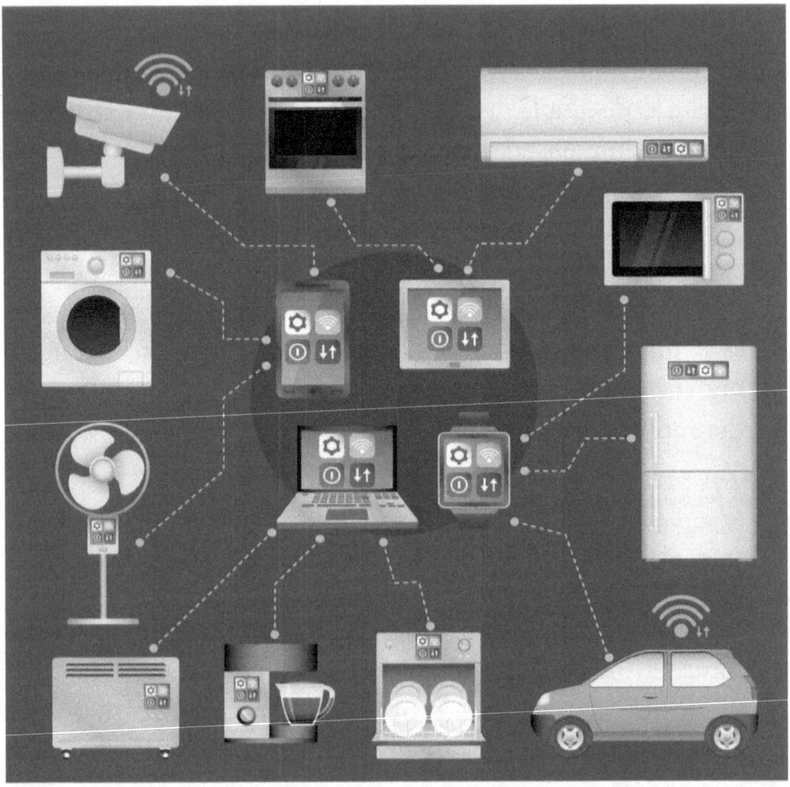

The IoT connects devices of all kinds, from refrigerators and washing machines to thermostats and self-driving cars.

refrigerators and washing machines to light bulbs, autonomous cars, and even rubber ducks.

The first reported instance of a coordinated suite of intelligent appliances occurred in 1979, when MicroAge founders

Jeff McKeever and Alan Hald held a press conference to demonstrate "Fred the House" and "Albert the Office." Based upon Apple computers with voice recognition software and remote control interfaces, the twin systems allowed a human to operate room lighting, appliances, drapery, and office machines using voice commands. Whereas these early systems were based on direct connections between the devices and a local computer, IoT devices rely on the internet to relay commands from the user's smartphone, or from the device itself, to a network server, which in turn activates the connected thermostat, light bulb, garage door opener, or rubber duck.

For example, an AI-empowered refrigerator, upon detecting a shortage of milk or eggs, might send the relevant information by email to the nearest grocery store. In 2014, a hacked smart refrigerator sent unsolicited messages to routers, multimedia centers, smart TVs and other smart refrigerators. From December 23 to January 6, email messages were sent three times per day in batches of 100,000 in the first Internet of Things cyberattack. Such attacks have since become commonplace. To illustrate the gravity of the risk, a virus called Stuxnet was able to decommission uranium enrichment centrifuges with ease.

U.S. Defense Secretary Leon Panetta warned that the United States is vulnerable to a "cyber Pearl Harbor" in which trains will be derailed, water supplies poisoned, and power grids crippled. Within a month, Chevron confirmed that it had become the first U.S. corporation to have its computers inflected with the Stuxnet virus. Security specialists have also demonstrated that the SCADA system of an oil-well pumping station can be easily hacked, with potentially catastrophic consequences.

It has been demonstrated with much publicity that any car or truck with an internet connection can be hacked by means of almost any WiFi-equipped device. An ominous threat is posed by drones with WiFi connections, capable of hacking and taking control of virtually any device, or infecting it with a cybervirus.

In 2011, security researcher Jay Radcliffe revealed that medical devices, such as an insulin pump, can be hacked and the attacker can alter the dosage and schedule of the insulin release. Even pacemakers can be invaded, enabling an attacker to perform mass murder. The Food and Drug Administration has issued a warning that medicine infusion pumps are vulnerable to cyberattack. Despite these red flags, thousands of critical medical systems, from MRI machines to X-ray machines remain sitting ducks for the sinister.

In December, 2015, hacks and database leaks related to internet-connected *Hello Kitty*, *Hello Barbie*, and other VTech toys placed millions of users at risk. The VTech hack exposed data of nearly five million parents and over 200,000 records for children, including thousands of photos of children and their parents. The *Hello Kitty* attack compromised the private information of 3.3 million users. The records exposed included first and last names, birthday, gender, country of origin, email addresses, password hint questions and the corresponding answers, and other data.

Security expert Matt Jakubowski was able to hack into Mattel's internet-connected *Hello Barbie*, gaining access to user information, stored MP3 audio files, and even the microphone. "You can take that information and find out a person's house or business," Jakubowski told NBC. "It's just a matter of time until we are able to replace their servers with ours and have her say anything we want."

John McAfee, addressing a computer security conference in May, 2016, insisted that the camera and microphones built into smartphones pose a serious threat to security and privacy. McAfee founded the iconic provider of antivirus protection McAfee Associates in 1987. Intel bought the firm for $7.7 billion in 2010. In his speech, McAfee insisted that it is relatively "trivial" for a hacker to remotely and secretly turn on a phone's sensors. Pointing to repeated cyber attacks on American infrastructure by foreign interests, he opined that neither the U.S. government nor the largest businesses appreciate how quickly society would collapse if large portions of the country lost power for even a few days. He offered this warning:

> *"We are teetering on an edge, not just as companies, not just as individuals, but as a nation and even as a world. We depend so much on our information science...this will be the new paradigm... and until you are touched, you do not understand the fullness of the risk."*

Fortunately for rubber duck lovers, to date *Edwin*, the internet-connected rubber duck, has yet to be hacked.

It has been predicted that, by 2020, 25 billion devices will be connected to the internet, and by 2025, a trillion. Already, there are 4.9 billion devices in the IoT, including smart home-automation devices, consumer products such as smart watches and health monitors, vehicles, and smart infrastructure used in buildings and cities. Unfortunately, virtually any device that can be connected to the internet is vulnerable.

It has been established by security specialists that, by hacking a kitchen appliance, a hacker could penetrate the entire residence, including its thermostat, garage door opener, automobile, and office. If, for example, the homeowner worked at a bank, the hacker would then be able to attack the bank and, thereby, the entire international banking system.

Security researchers Runa Sandvik and Michael Auger discovered that a computer-controlled sniper rifle is vulnerable to cyberattack via its WiFi connections. The scope's calculations can be altered so that the shooter misses the target or shoots a different target. Software intruders can also disable the scope's computer or even prevent the weapon from firing. The shooter would not even be aware that the rifle had been hacked.

Of little comfort, power grids are also part of the Internet of Things and as vulnerable as a refrigerator, car, or *Barbie* doll. Richard Burr, a U.S. Senator from North Carolina said,

> *"We often take for granted that our lights will come on when we flip the light switch, but the reality is that our reliability standards and the current state of the transmission grid leave us all vulnerable to blackouts."*

Infrastructure Vulnerability

Software running on a computer connected to an Uninterrupted Power Supply (UPS) or a backup battery will survive an ordinary blackout. A long-term failure of the electrical grid would snuff out any form of AI—at least until its software is reloaded on a sufficiently powered machine.

On a global level, power grids are most vulnerable to the threat of solar storms. The most powerful solar storms send coronal mass ejections (CMEs), containing charged particles, into space. If the earth happens to be in a CME's path, the charged particles are capable of disrupting satellites in orbit—

or even causing them to fail—as well as disrupting telecommunications and navigation systems of high-flying aircraft. They have the potential to affect power grids, and have been known to black out entire cities, even entire regions.

In 1989, a solar storm caused a power failure that spanned Quebec and the northeastern United States, leaving over six million people without electricity for nine hours. Far more powerful solar storms are not only possible but inevitable.

According to the National Academy of Sciences, a monstrous blast of geomagnetic particles from the sun could destroy 300 or more of the 2,100 high-voltage transformers that are the backbone of the U.S. electric grid. Even a few hundred destroyed transformers could disable the entire interconnected system. Although the likelihood of a solar storm of such magnitude occurring in just the next decade may be relatively low, the impact would be both disastrous and costly.

About 365 high-voltage transformers in the continental United States are at risk of failure or permanent damage in the event of a solar superstorm. Replacements for transformers might not be available for a year or more, and the cost of damage in the first year after the storm would reach two trillion dollars. The national grid was built over decades to deliver energy as cost effectively as possible from the point of generation. A solar superstorm has the capacity to bring the entire network down. In short, as civilization becomes increasingly dependent on electronic devices, it will become inexorably more vulnerable to both natural and human influences affecting the power grid.

Stunning AI breakthroughs leading to sensient robots or the feasibility of mind transference are ultimately predicated not on "Moore's Law" but on "Voltaire's Law:" the illusion that everything is fine, not just today, but until the outer limits of the imagination.

Estimated Global IoT Expenditures

Year	***$ (Billions)***
2014	939
2016	1414
2018	2060
2020	3010

16

Rules of Engagement

AI Legality and Ethics

"Life can only be understood backwards; but it must be lived forwards."
Søren Kierkegaard

If all humans shared a universal ethical standard, it would be reasonable to assume that cognitive computers and sensient robots, would inherit—whether by design or acquisition—human ethical behavior. Indeed, some philosophers have mused that a computer reproducing a human brain in exact detail would automatically acquire human ethical sensibilities. However, ethical standards are far from universal, as history has proved repeatedly.

As Fyodor Dostoevsky, whose writings provided the basis of existentialist philosophy, contended, "within every heart is the capacity for infinite good, but also unfathomable evil." While imprisoned in a labor camp in Siberia, he observed that even criminals convicted of the most heinous crimes justified their actions, from their own points of view, as moral and just. The same, undoubtedly, is true today, not only of many criminals, but also of ideological extremists, terrorists, and politicians.

Ethics and Evolution

The origin, development, and embrace of ethical standards emerged from evolutionary pressures; were ethical sensibilities not of positive adaptive value, humans would not possess them and, undoubtedly, would not have survived to this point. The evolution of human intelligence simultaneous to the quest for morality were the most influential events in the rise of Homo Sapiens. As the civilizations and cultures spawned by that intelligence multiplied, moral definitions diversified.

One often reads that all humans share a common intrinsic ethical sensibility. The problem is that there is no common definition or expression of what constitutes ethics or morality. Human history is a never-ending saga of war inspired by conflicting ethical standards and belief systems.

Some Singularity followers and philosophy teachers have espoused that building an exact electronic replica of a human brain will automatically create consciousness and, with it, the same ethical tendencies as a human. What is meant by those who embrace this hypothesis is "the same ethical tendencies that I have."

It is dangerously ingenuous to believe that any such tendencies that automatically appear in a self-aware computer would parallel those of a Singularity follower—or, for that matter, of any particular belief system or culture.

As described in Chapter 13, Chomsky described the innate basis of language, "Mentalese," which precedes the development of the mind from birth. A similar innate behavior, which we might similarly call "Moralese," is expressed by every brain as it emerges from its egocentric shell. Like language, moral expressions are acquired from the environment and, as such, take shape as a result of family, cultural, environmental, intellectual, and emotional influences. Just as language is both acquired by experience and learned from instruction, the subjective moral and ethical standards we develop from birth to adolescence are also cultivated by our environment.

The Ethical Challenge

The only way cognitive computers can acquire ethical sensibilities is by instruction. Consequently, every AI-empowered machine—whether an autonomous weapon, robotic surgeon, surrogate lawyer, Virtual Reality device, or internet-connected rubber duck—will inherit either the ethical values of its software developer or none at all. Nothing could be more naive than the premise that a sensient computer equivocal to the mind of a human would "inherit" benign ethical sensibilities. As history—and civilization as it now exists—demonstrate conclusively, "benign" is a subjective value. A suicide bomber's ethical sensibilities are as deeply ingrained in his or her consciousness as those of a Red Cross volunteer.

Simply stated, ethical disparity is the most formidable obstacle to creating ethical AI. In Western philosophy, ethical behavior is most likely to be considered to consist of actions and attitudes that strive to promote truthfulness, honesty, and the toleration of others. In some Asian and Middle Eastern cultures, the end is more likely to be seen as justifying the means; if the end is just, deception or coercion are apt to be considered irrelevant.

The diverse influence of belief systems on ethical behavior is clearly at odds with the notion of a universal standard of ethics. As the Greek philosopher Epicurus postulated, "No one who sees evil deliberately chooses it, but is enticed by it as being good in comparison with a greater evil and therefore pursues it."

Terrorism is rooted not just in religious fervor, but also on biological forces inherited from our evolutionary origins, when the killing instinct proved to be of positive adaptive value. Ironically, ethical sensibilities emerged as a mitigating influence on the killing instinct, but now pose a nearly equal threat to survival. Nevertheless, no one involved in AI research and development doubts that ethical standards of some sort must be adopted.

The Standards Debate

Historically, governments have attempted to mitigate the inherently barbaric nature of waging war through "rules of engagement," based on the Western European premise of a "higher morality" prescribed by governments, religions, and educational institutions. The premise disintegrated in the face of opposing moralities, such as those expressed by fanatical, nihilist, and anti-government terrorists in both hemispheres.

International humanitarian laws that govern attacks on humans in times of war have no specific provisions for autonomous weapons. The 1949 Geneva Convention on humane conduct in war requires any attack to satisfy three criteria: military necessity, discrimination between combatants and non-combatants, and proportionality between the value of the military objective and the potential for collateral damage. The Martens Clause, added in 1977, bans weapons that violate the "principles of humanity and the dictates of public conscience."

Germany and Japan have advocated for a total ban on autonomous weapons systems, whereas the United States, the

United Kingdom and Israel—the leading developers of AI-empowered weaponry—oppose such a treaty. The debate is multi-faceted. Proponents maintain that "ethical" autonomous weapons can minimize civilian casualties by targeting only combatants. Opponents fear that self-guided killing machines will make wars more likely. Unquestionably, AI weaponry ending up in the hands of terrorists and rogue nations has potentially catastrophic consequences.

In relation to international law, an important question will inevitably be asked: Does the deployment of AI weapons constitute a war crime? The issue is framed around the concept of "collateral damage"—a term first used during the Vietnam War to describe noncombatant casualties and damage. Attacks that are expected to cause collateral damage are not prohibited *per se*, but the laws of armed conflict restrict indiscriminate attacks. Article 57 of the 1977 Additional Protocol I to the Geneva Conventions states that, in an international conflict, "constant care shall be taken to spare the civilian population, civilians, and civilian objects."

An indiscriminate attack also includes using means and methods that cannot be directed at specific military objectives or whose effects cannot be limited. An autonomous weapon that seeks and destroys targets indiscriminately would clearly constitute a violation. A self-guided weapon ostensibly programmed to target only enemy combatants would not. On the other hand, terrorists ignore the Geneva Convention and disdain international law.

The options are either to ban AI weapons altogether or to attempt to regulate their use through international treaties. Considering it is highly unlikely, if not impossible, to ban the continued development and deployment of autonomous killing machines, a framework for international regulation, similar to the Geneva Convention, is the best possible outcome. AI expert input will be needed in establishing any framework because of the complexity of the field and the general lack of understanding outside the AI research and development community. Advisory committees to legislatures and governments should be established sooner rather than later.

It is essential that discussions about AI ethical methodologies should be organized at scientific meetings, as well as popular science events. Research and opinion papers devoted to AI ethics must be published on a broad scale, to engage the public in the conversation. Doing nothing is a vote in favor of thinking machine chaos.

On a design level, built-in safeguards, limitations, and "kill switches" are obvious requirements, but, pragmatically, there is no reason to believe such measures will be adopted by all parties wishing to deploy such weapons. In manufacturing and marketing, ethics are commonly sacrificed for expediency.

Designing a Blueprint for Survival

Beyond the AI arms race, cognitive computing is already affecting you on a more personal level than you may realize. From the vulnerability of the Internet of Things (IoT) to the specter of AI-related job losses, the life of everyone alive today is being transformed, for better or worse.

The most fundamental thing you can do to survive in the era of thinking machine chaos, as simple as it may seem, is to take basic precautions to secure yourself and your family.

The most prominent threat posed by IoT devices is their inherent vulnerability. As the number of smart devices implemented by consumers and businesses expands, the likelihood of new threats also grows. The diversion of smart devices to conduct espionage and sabotage is already commonplace. Smart locks installed in hotels can be unlocked by an electronic master key. Internet-connected pacemakers, insulin pumps, and other medical devices are no less vulnerable than smart refrigerators, toilet paper holders, and baby monitors. Any patient's medical records and personal information can be accessed, sold, or even altered.

The development of connected devices is accelerating, but security issues are largely being ignored. An ineffective—or nonexistent—plan for deploying security updates will be the most serious vulnerability. Software manufacturers must be prepared to quickly respond to security breaches and release updates to protect their users. Unfortunately, patching vulnerabilities on internet-connected devices is presently a very low priority for manufacturers. Most likely, any updates will be available only when new versions of the devices are purchased, leaving existing products perpetually vulnerable.

Presently, the majority of attacks on interconnected devices involve weak password protection. In fact, two-thirds of such devices are installed by users with the default password contained in the manufacturer's instructions.

Amazingly, the most common passwords adopted by users of internet-connected devices are "password", "password1", "123456", "Ashley," "baseball," and "jesus." It's hardly puzzling that such devices are easily hacked, even by amateurs.

On a personal level, the simplest measure to guard against cyber espionage is to create a hard-to-crack password. Unfortunately, given enough time, any password can be cracked by brute force using password-hacking software. A typical desktop PC is capable of trying tens of millions of character combinations per second. Nevertheless, an obscure password significantly reduces vulnerability to a mass attack on a large number of similar devices.

The Eight Commandments of Password Security

Password security can be optimized by adhering to eight basic commandments:

1. Thou shalt not use a valid word as a password. Words can easily be cracked using a dictionary as a database.

2. Thou shalt not use a calendar date as a password. People tend to use dates that are meaningful to them, such as birthdays or anniversaries, which any hacker can determine with a little biographical research.

3. Thou shalt use lower and upper case letters, digits, and one or more special symbols such as *!*, #, or *%*.

4. Thy password shall consist of eight to fifteen characters. Fewer than eight characters are relatively easy to hack.

5. Thou shalt never share thy password with anyone else.

6. Thou shalt never write down or store a password where it could be found by a snooper.

7. Thou shalt change thy password regularly, at least once every six months.

8. Thou shalt not recycle a password after replacing it with a different one.

From a manufacturer's perspective, an essential method of optimizing IoT security is to implement a private network with private IP ranges and restricted access. Unfortunately, fewer than two percent of the manufacturers of IoT products do so.

Ultimately, government regulation of advanced AI-empowered machines must be regarded as an essential process, especially the development and enforcement of rigorous safety standards. New laws are already needed to determine issues of legal liability. If an autonomous police drone targeting a terrorist kills innocent bystanders, or if a self-driving car runs over a pedestrian while swerving to avoid an accident, who is at fault—the manufacturer, engineer, programmer, or owner? Without substantial changes to existing laws, it's possible all the parties—or none—might be held liable. If a person dies on the operating table while attempting to have his or her mind uploaded to a computer, is it medical malpractice, assisted suicide, negligent manslaughter, or defective product liability?

Laws creating strict liability for harm or damage caused by defective products already exist in many places. However, is an AI system really defective if it performs according to its design, even if the results are unintended? Often, negligence must be proved to establish liability. Can an AI system be considered negligent for following the instructions of its programming and architecture? All these questions must be addressed by new laws, before actual cases occur.

Regulation of automated stock trading systems is also inevitable. Already, decisions made by computers produce instant and dramatic fluctuations in stock prices, often with little or no relation to the actual financial health of the issuing company or general economic trends.

From both practical and legal standpoints, no attempt to regulate AI as a category is likely to succeed. The problem is that there is no specific, commonly accepted definition of what constitutes AI, even among scientists, engineers, and programmers working in the field. To determine liability resulting from the actions of an autonomous system requires naming the specific entities in question, not their general characteristics or software architecture.

For example, regulations could be adopted for "self-driving cars" without a description of their specific hardware and software components. An "autonomous" system can be defined in general terms as a product based on computer hardware and software that both function and make decisions independently of human guidance or interference. Whether or not such a product exhibits human-like cognition or is capable of learning new behavior based on experience—issues that legal experts often haggle over—is largely irrelevant. The main concern is regulating devices that are intended to perform autonomously, whether a semi-truck, drone, boat, or sexbot.

Some legal experts have speculated that unexpected behavior by an AI system could result in a verdict of no liability, since the effects were unforeseeable. Regulations must specifically target the foreseeability issue to seal potential loopholes that would surely be exploited by abusers of the system.

Nevertheless, legal mechanisms are essential to reduce the public risks related to AI systems. Such mechanisms can be formulated and implemented without stifling innovation. Many of the problems are no more than ambiguities, omissions, and shortcomings that can be resolved by precise definitions and targeted regulations.

From a legislative standpoint, regulation will be more difficult to achieve, due to the inherent nature of the process and lack of AI expertise. Whereas expert witnesses are available to courts, legislatures are prone to consulting lobby groups and catering to special interests or their constituencies, when considering new laws. No matter what form regulation takes, it will be impossible to enforce globally. Whatever can be done, no matter what the consequences, will be done by someone. The most immediate risks of AI are error or terror.

Left to their own devices, lawyers, policymakers, scientists, ethicists, lawyers, businesses, financial institutions, military leaders, and ethicists would draft very different rules. Nevertheless, collaboration between all will be essential.

It's unreasonable to anticipate a consensus of opinion on AI regulation. As with climate change, famine, genetically modified organisms, nuclear weapons, human rights, and similar global issues, the best we can hope for is a loose framework to which the majority of nations agree. Nevertheless, such a framework is the best outcome that can be expected.

Will subjective "ethical programming," governmental regulation, and liability laws be enough to quell thinking machine chaos? If history has taught us anything, such measures will prove to be ineffectual in preventing a new era of AI-related litigation, wartime atrocities, infrastructure failures, and criminal and terrorist acts. Still, the measures will be as necessary to the maintenance of the semblance of civilization as nuclear weapons treaties and the Geneva Convention.

Richard Stallman, known for having created the GNU software environment, observed, "Whether gods exist or not, there is no way to get absolute certainty about ethics. Without absolute certainty, we do the best we can."

AI Survival Mandates

Personal
Use hard-to-decrypt passwords
Avoid devices that lack advanced security
Litigate against AI failures
Vote to regulate AI-empowered products
Corporate
Integrate maximum security in IoT devices
Use private networks
Assess AI risks and establish risk management policies
Regulatory
Require IoT manufacturers to integrate security
Implement oversight of AI stock trading
Establish rules of engagement for AI weapons
Educational
Teach ethical responsibility in classrooms
Promote cross-cultural understanding
Global
Establish and enforce an AI Weapons Convention

EPILOG

We live not only in a time of social and technological transition, but also of biological, evolutionary, and environmental transition. It is also a time of great and growing upheaval—by social classes, species, and the planet itself.

Artificial intelligence has already permeated many aspects of daily life and will continue to alter the affairs of men and women, institutions, and warfare, for better and worse, beyond the lifetime of anyone reading these words.

Of all the traits that contributed to the rise and eventual dominance of humankind, ingenuity was perhaps the most profound. Yet, it is our very rise and dominance that produced the coming clash between civilization and chaos. In the end, our ingenuity may prove to be our demise or our salvation.

As Charles Darwin discovered in the Galapagos Islands, "It is not the strongest of the species that survives, nor the most intelligent... It is the one that is the most adaptable to change."

Whether from brain-computer interfaces, routine interaction with superintelligent machines, bioenhancement, or the impact of autonomous weapons, the lives of everyone born from this point forward will inexorably be affected by the spread of artificial intelligence.

On an individual level, AI will provide the means to improve memory and cognition, expand the physical senses, and interact with an ever-growing array of "smart" devices and gadgets. Inevitably, the distinction between humanity and technology will become increasingly blurred. Every product spawned by AI developments—from brain implants to weaponry—will likely be available for purchase on the open market, as well as unsanctioned "gray" and "black" markets. As is the nature of all manufactured products, every smart, semi-smart, intelligent, or superintelligent device will be subject to design flaws, engineering mistakes, manufacturing problems, breakdowns, and obsolescence.

Some devices will be superior to others, more elaborate, expensive, and, therefore more prestigious, much the same as various brands of automobiles and apparel are today. Brain implants, cybernetic limbs, and self-flying drones will become status symbols, common among those who can afford them, but financially beyond the reach of ordinary working people.

A profound but overlooked sociological impact of AI is the potential for the de-humanization of society. Merged with the superintelligent machines that shape their new reality, humans risk becoming manufactured things themselves, reduced to the sum total of their modified traits, interfaces, enhancements, and gadgetry. Society already exerts enormous pressure, through advertising, entertainment, and social media, to continually strive for achievement, competitive advantage, and re-invention. At every juncture, we are cajoled to be ever more attractive, interesting, and affluent—in other words, to be constantly dissatisfied with ourselves, our possessions, and our surroundings.

As civilization continues to increase its dependency on technology, opting out will not be part of the discussion. It's one thing to have a tatoo removed, another altogether to have a brain implant disconnected. At some point, humanity becomes a "platform," comparable to a computer's operating system, for the installation of performance-boosting enhancements. Personality traits then become "features", abilities become "assets," and shortcomings "liabilities."

The less humanized we become organically, the more we must adjust our attitudes toward what constitutes humanity. It is not enough to raise children to compete in a technologically advanced society, teach them to perform perfunctory skills, and motivate them to be thinner, smarter, and better looking. As wards of the future, we must also help future generations understand social, organizational, and technological systems; make ethical decisions; apply their knowledge to meaningful tasks; and work, communicate, and interact with people from culturally diverse backgrounds.

We who are alive now may well constitute the last purely human society. As such, we must somehow act in concert to achieve a universal commitment to lifelong learning, cooperation, and the dedication to the highest standards of behavior, not only in our private lives, but in all aspects of personal endeavor.

AI GLOSSARY

AI Agent Any device empowered by AI software.

Algorithm A predefined sequence of procedures, expressed in plain language, to produce a desired outcome.

Analytics The logical science of analysis.

Artificial Intelligence (AI) Computer software that mimics or duplicates human cognition.

Artificial Neural Network (ANN) A computer system using processors as "neurons" and circuits as "synapses" to process data, inspired by the architecture of a human brain.

Associative Memory The recollection of complete memories from partial information.

Autonomous Capable of operating independently without human intervention or a ruling entity.

Brain-Computer Interface (BCI) A direct connection between a human brain and a computer, created by electrodes implanted in the brain, or by a noninvasive means such as an MRI scanner or EEG.

Braingate The linking of two or more brains via implanted electrodes.

Case-Based Reasoning (CBR) The formation of logical conclusions based on the outcomes of documented cases.

Connectome A map, similar to a circuit diagram, of the anatomical and functional connectivity of the human brain.

DARPA Defense Advanced Research Project Agency.

Data The plural of datum, referring to any item of information, such as a fact, statement, formula, product, etc.

Data Mining The use of analytics to collect, analyze, and form conclusions from a continuously growing body of data.

Deduction A statement or argument consisting of a premise that results in a conclusion.

Deductive Reasoning The formation of conclusions based on cause-effect relationships.

Denial of Service An attack on an internet website or computer network to block access by users, typically by submitting more requests than the system can accommodate.

Deep Learning A method of expanding databases based on acquisition of new data, mimicking a human "learning from experience."

Domain An area of expertise; in AI programming, a category of expressions with common properties.

Expert System A computer system that mimics human reasoning using the heuristic processes that underly problem solving by a human expert.

Fire and Forget An autonomous weapon that tracks, targets, and fires on a predefined objective without human guidance or intervention.

Fuzzy Logic A method of processing data based on variable information, especially used in image recognition and natural language processing.

Haptic Devices, such as gloves or suits, designed to interact with a Virtual Reality immersion using touch and response to weight or force.

Hedonic Relating to the production of pleasure.

Heuristics The science of defining cause-effect relationships based on human problem solving techniques.

Hierarchical Reasoning The process by which cause-effect relationships are formed based on observation and experience, rather than detailed logical analysis.

Humane Genome Project A working-draft sequence of all the genes in a human body, known collectively as the genome.

If-Then Rule A logical statement based on a cause-effect relationship, consisting of a predicate ("If" component) and a conclusion ("Then" component).

Inference The process of forming conclusions based on facts or evidence.

Inference Engine In an expert system, software that processes if-then rules in the context of a specific knowledge base.

Intelligent Agent Any system containing AI programming.

internet of Things (IoT) A term used to describe devices of all kinds connected to the internet.

Knowledge Base A database consisting of facts derived from the knowledge of human experts in a particular field.

Knowledge Engineering The process of extracting, organizing, and storing knowledge from a human expert.

Knowledge Representation The translation of human expertise into if-then rules capable of being processed by an expert system.

Machine Learning The process of expanding a database with new information obtained autonomously by a computer.

Moore's Law Slang for the speculation that the number of circuits that can be compressed on a circuit board will double every year, indefinitely, based on an essay by Gordon Moore.

Natural Language Processing The recognition and encoding of plain language by a computer.

Neural Computing Data processing based on the use of computer processors as "neurons" and electric circuits as "synapses," inspired by the architecture of human brains.

Neuron A type of brain cell that transmits and receives electrochemical messages, responsible for cognition, sensory interpretation, and retention of memories.

Pattern Recognition The matching by a computer of external patterns, such as images or sounds, with information stored in a database or accessible via a network.

Qualitative Reasoning The process of forming conclusions based on physical qualities rather than predefined facts.

Quant A hacker who utilizes AI software to manipulate the Stock Market.

Quote Stuffing The use of AI software to launch a Denial of Service attack on stock trading.

Rule-based System Expert system.

Schema The representation of knowledge in a machine-readable format.

Shallow Knowledge Data derived from the heuristic processes used by a human expert to solve problems.

Singularity A hypothetical point in human history when computers will become sensient beings of equal or superior intelligence to humans.

Syllogism In logic, a statement in which the conclusion directly follows from its premise; the expression of a cause-effect relationship.

Transhumanism A belief system based on the pursuit of a future technology enabling a human mind to be transferred to a computer or robot.

Turing Test A hypothetical test defined by Alan Turing to determine a computer's ability to mimic human reasoning, using natural language.

Virtual Reality (VR) An interactive sensory simulation experienced in a three-dimensional environment.

BIBLIOGRAPHY

Aleksander, I, *Designing Intelligent Systems: An Introduction*, Kogan Page, 1984.

Amato, Ivan and Lewin, Sarah et al, "Artificial Intelligence Aligned with Human Values," *Quanta Magazine*, April 21, 2015.

Angelova, Kamelia, "How Robots Have Evolved Over The Last 200 Years," *Business Insider*, July 6, 2011.

Arkertkar, Rajendra, *Introduction to Artificial Intelligence*, PHI Learning, 2014.

Asimov, Isaac and Frenkel, Karen, *Robots: Machines in Man's Image*, Harmony Books, 1985.

Autor, D. and Dorn, D., "The Growth of Low-Skill Service Jobs and the Polarization of the US Labor Market." *American Economic Review*, 2013.

Baker, Natasha, "Emerging Technologies Every Office Will Have In \ 2020," *Forbes*, May 21, 2013.

Barrat, James, *Our Final Invention: Artificial Intelligence and the End of the Human Era*, St. Martin's Griffin, 2013.

Bennett, C. C. and Hauser, K., "Artificial Intelligence Framework for Simulating Clinical Decision-Making: A Markov Decision Process Approach," *Artificial Intelligence in Medicine*, 2013.

Berlinski, David, *The Advent of the Algorithm*, Harcourt Books, 2000.

Berridge, Kent and Kringelbach, Morten, "Affective Neuroscience of Pleasure: Reward in Humans and Animals," *Psychopharmacology*, 2008.

Bickhard, M. H. and Terveen, L., *Foundational Issues in Artificial Intelligence and Cognitive Science: Impasse and Solution*, Elsevier.

Bishop, C.M., *Neural Networks for Pattern Recognition*, Oxford University Press, 1995.

Bloom P., *How Pleasure Works*, W. W. Norton & Co, 2010.

Bostrom, Nick, "Existential Risks: Analyzing Human Extinction Scenarios and Related Hazards," *Journal of Evolution and Technology*, 2002.

Bostrom, Nick, *Superintelligence: Paths, Dangers, Strategies*, Oxford University Press, 2014.

Bostrom, N. and Yudkowsky, E. *The Ethics of Artificial Intelligence*, Cambridge University Press, Cambridge, 2013

Bowler, Tim, "Killer robots: Are They Really Inevitable?" *BBC News*, May 21, 2014.

Braga, Newton, *Robotics, Mechatronics, and Artificial Intelligence*, Elsevier, 2001.

Brumson, Bennett, *Chemical and Hazardous Material Handling Robotics*, Robotic Industries Association, January 18, 2007.

Buchanan, B. G., et al., "An Application of Artificial Intelligence to the Interpretation of Mass Spectra," *Mass Spectrometry: Techniques and Applications*, Wiley-Interscience, New York, 1971.

Buchanan, B. G. and Shortliffe, E. H., "Model-Based Learning of Production Rules," *Pattern Directed Inference Systems*, Academic Press, New York, 1978.

Buchanan, B. G. and Shortliffe, E. H., *Rule Based Expert Systems*, Addison-Wesley, Reading, MA, 1984.

Buckner R., et al., "The Brain's Default Network: Anatomy, Function, and Relevance to Disease," *Annals of the New York Academy of Sciences*, 2008.

Butter, M., Rensma, A., van Boxsel, J. et al., *Robotics for Healthcare Final Report*, European Commission, DG Information Society, 2008.

Chalmers, David, "Facing Up to the Problem of Consciousness," *Journal of Consciousness Studies*, 1995.

Chambers, John, ed., *The Oxford Companion to American Military History* Oxford University Press, 1999.

Chomsky, Noam, *Aspects of the Theory of Syntax*, Cambridge, MA, MIT Press, 1965

Chomsky, Noam (1975), *Logical Structure of Linguistic Theory, The,* Plenum, New York, 1975

Chomsky, Noam, *Syntactic Structures*, Mouton, The Hague, 1957

Ciresan,D. et al, "Deep Neural Networks Segment Neuronal Membranes in Electron Microscopy Images," *Advances in Neural Information Processing Systems*, 2012.

Coombs,R., *Nanotechnology in Medicine and the Biosciences*, Gordon & Breach Press, 2005.

Danaher, John, "Is Regulation of Artificial Intelligence Possible?," *Hplus Magazine*, July 15, 2015.

Datteri, E., & Tamburrini, G., "Ethical Reflections on Healthcare Robotics," *Istituto Nazionale di Fisica Nucleare.*

DeAngelis, Stephen, "Artificial Intelligence and Human Brains," Enterra Solutions, June, 2012.

"Deep Belief Networks," *Scholarpedia.*

Defense Advanced Research Projects Agency (DARPA)

Diana, A., "Twelve Advances in Medical Robotics," *Information Week*, January 29, 2011.

Drescher, Gary L., *Good and Real: Demystifying Paradoxes from Physics to Ethics*, MIT Press, 2006.

Duda, R. O., et al., "Semantic Network Representations in Rule-Based Inference Systems," *Pattern-Directed Inference Systems*, Academic Press, Menlo Park, 1977.

Dyer, Geoff, "U.S. Military: Robot Wars," *Financial Times*, February 7, 2016.

Ford, M., *Rise of the robots: Technology and the Threat of a Jobless Future*, Basic Books, New York, 2015.

Foster, Dennis L., *Designing Intelligent Databases*, Auerbach, 1985.

Foster, Dennis L., *Programming with AI Languages*, Auerbach, 1985.

Franklin, Stanley P. *Artificial Minds*, MIT Press, Cambridge, MA, 1995.

Frey, C. B., *The Future of Employment: How Susceptible Are Jobs to Computerisation?*, 2013.

Frijda N., *On the Nature and Function of Pleasure, Pleasures of the Brain*, Oxford University Press, 2010.

Ghose, Tia, "Intelligent Robots Will Overtake Humans by 2100, Experts Say," *Science*, May 7, 2013.

Gray, Patrick, "Artificial Intelligence: Know Its Purported Benefits and Risks," *Tech Republic*, January 5, 2015.

Green A. et al, "Neural Signatures in Patients with Neuropathic Pain," *Neurology*, 2009.

Hall, Owen P., "Artificial Intelligence Techniques Enhance Business Forecasts," *Graziadio Business Review*, Pepperdine University, October 8, 2010.

Harmon, P. and King, D., *Artificial Intelligence in Business*, John Wiley and Sons, New York, 1985.

Hay, Maciamo, "Mind Uploading Won't Lead to Immortality," *Vita Modularis*, April 19, 2014.

Hidalgo, Cesar, *Why Information Grows: The Evolution of Order from Atoms to Economics*, Basic Books, 2015.

Hinton, G. E. et al, "A Fast Learning Algorithm for Deep Belief Nets," *Neural Computation*, National Institutes of Health, 2006.

Hiremath, Shivayogi et al, *Brain Computer Interface Learning for Systems Based on Electrocorticography and Intracortical Microelectrode Arrays*, National Institutes of Health, 2015.

Hoffman, Mark, "Scientists Grow Human Brain Tissue in Test Tubes," *World Science Report*, August 30, 2013.

"How Artificial Intelligence Will Revolutionize Our Lives ," *National Geographic*, October, 2015.

Howard-Jones, et al., "Neuroeducational Research in the Design and Use of a Learning Technology," *Learning, Media and Technology*, 2014.

Ilyin, Yuri, "Internet of Things: Vulnerability and Security," *Kapersky Lab Business*, February 13, 2014.

Indiveri, Giacomo, "Microships Mimic Brain's Processing Power," *Discovery*, 2013.

Ivanova, Olga et al., "Additive Manufacturing and Nanotechnology: Promises and Challenges," *Rapid Prototyping Journal*, 2013.

Jahnke, Art, *History and Future of Funding for Scientific Research*, Boston University.

Kahn, Kenneth, *Three Interactions Between AI and Education*, MIT AI Laboratory.

Kai, K., "Nanotechnology and Medical Robotics; Legal and Ethical Resposibility," *Waseda*, December 5, 2012.

Kaplan, Jerry, *Humans Need Not Apply: A Guide to Wealth and Work in the Age of Artificial Intelligence*, Yale University Press, 2015.

Kaufman, Roy, "How Traders Are Using Text and Data Mining to Beat the Market," *The Street*, February 12, 2015.

Kirk, Jeremy, "Coming Soon to your Smart TV: The Next Wave of Cybercrime," *Computerworld*, December 28, 2015.

Kodratoff, Yves and Michalski Ryszard, *Machine Learning: An Artificial Intelligence Approach*, Elsevier, 2014.

Korolov, Maria, "The Real Risks of Virtual Reality," *Risk Management*, October 1, 2014.

Kringelbach, Morten, "The Human Orbitofrontal Cortex: Linking Reward to Hedonic Experience," *Nature Reviews Neuroscience*, 2005.

Kringelbach, Morten, "Emotion," *The Oxford Companion to the Mind*, Oxford University Press, 2004.

Kurzweil, *The Singularity Is Near: When Humans Transcend Biology*, Penguin Books, 2005.

Langton, C.G. et al, "Artificial Life II," *SFI Studies in the Sciences of Complexity*, Addison-Wesley, Redwood City, CA, 1992.

Laszlo, E., "The Connectivity Hypothesis: Foundations of an Integral Science of Quantum," *Cosmos*.

Laureys S., et al, "Brain function in Coma, Vegetative State, and Related Disorders," *Lancet*, 2004.

Lindsay, Robert K., et al., "Dendral: A Case Study of the First Expert System for Scientific Hypothesis Information," *Artificial Intelligence*, Elsevier, New York, 1993.

Lindsay, Robert K., et al., *Applications of Artificial Intelligence for Organic Chemistry: The DENDRAL Project*, McGraw-Hill, New York, 1980.

Lloyd, Seth, "Computational Capacity of the Universe," *Physical Review Letters*, June 10, 2002.

Lohn, Andrew, et al., "How We Can Overcome the Risks of AI," *Time*, October 22, 2015.

Loubriel, Andres, "Artificial Intelligence Could Be Taking Over the Stock Market," *The Guardian*, June 15, 2014.

Luckin, R., *Re-designing Learning Contexts: Technology-Rich, Learner-Centred Ecologies*, Routledge, London, 2010.

Mabus Ray, *Prepared Remarks at Sea-Air-Space 2015*, U.S. Navy, April 15, 2015.

Maes, P. ed., *Designing Autonomous Agents*, Elsevier, 1990.

Markoff, John "Scientists See Promise in Deep-Learning Programs," *New York Times*, November 23, 2012.

Martin, Suzanne, *Virtual Reality in Medicine*, Worcester Polytechnic Institute, 1995.

Mayer-Schönberger, V., and Cukier, K. *Big data: A Revolution That Will Transform How We Live, Work, and Think*, Houghton Mifflin Harcourt, New York, 2013.

McVay, R., Moy, L. et al, "Killed by Code: Software Transparency in Implantable Medical Devices," *Software Freedom Law Center*.

"Medical Device Security Pacemakers, Other Implemented Devices, Vulnerable to Lethal Attacks," *Homeland Security Newswire*, November 28, 2012.

Muller, Vincent C., *Risks of Artificial Intelligence*, CRC Press, 2016. National Aeronautics and Space Administration

Nelson, Patrick, "Anatomy of an IoT Hack," *Network World*, August 28, 2015.

Newell, A. and Simon, H. A., *GPS, A Program that Simulates Human Thought, Computers and Thought*, McGraw-Hill, 1963.

Newell, A. and Simon, H. A., *Human Problem Solving*, Prentice-Hall, 1972.

Nobile, C., "Robots Vulnerable to Hacking," *Robotic Business Review*, August 20, 2012.

Norvig, Peter, *Paradigms of Artificial Intelligence Programming*, Elsevier, 2014.

Olsson, Magnus, "Nano-Brain-Implant Technologies and Artificial Intelligence," lecture, 2012.

"Open Source Medical Devices," *The Economist*, June 2, 2012.

Parksinon, John, "IoT mapped: The Emerging Landscape of Smart Things," *VentureBeat*, August 23, 2015.

Partridge, Derek, *A New Guide to Artificial Intelligence, Ablex*, 1991.

Paul, Annie Murphy, "The Machines Are Taking Over," *New York Times*, September 14, 2012.

Pham, D. T., "Neural Networks in Engineering, Applications of Artificial Intelligence in Engineering," *Computational Mechanics Publications*, 1994.

Poole, David and Mackworth, Alan, *Artificial Intelligence: Foundations of Computational Agents*, Cambridge University Press, 2010.

Porter, Stephen, "Virtual Reality", *Computer Graphics World*, March, 1992.

Rieland, Randy, "Mapping How the Brain Thinks," *Smithsonian*, February 25, 2013.

Russell, Stuart and Norvig, Peter, *Artificial Intelligence: A Modern Approach*, Prentice-Hall, 2010.

Russell, Stuart, "Take a Stand on AI Weapons," *Nature*, May 27, 2015.

Rzevski, *George, Artificial Intelligence in Engineering: Past, Present and Future*, American Institute of Engineers, 1995.

Sandberg, Anders, and Bostrom, Nick, *Whole Brain Emulation: A Roadmap*, University of Oxford, 2008

Sawyer, Brian and Foster, Dennis, *Programming Expert Systems in Modula II*, John Wiley and Sons, 1985.

Sawyer, Brian and Foster, Dennis, *Programming Expert Systems in Pascal*, John Wiley and Sons, 1985.

Seeman, Nadrian, "Nanotechnology and the Double Helix," *Scientific American*, June 2004.

Self, J., "The Defining Characteristics of Intelligent Tutoring Systems Research: ITSs Care, Precisely", *International Journal of Artificial Intelligence in Education*, 1999.

Shortliffe, E. H., *Computer-Based Medical Consultations: MYCIN*, Elsevier, New York, 1976.

Smith K., et al, "Hedonic Hotspots: Generating Sensory Pleasure in the Brain," *Pleasures of the Brain*, Oxford University Press, 2010.

Smith, Murray, *Neural Networks for Statistical Modeling*, Van Nostrand Reinhold, 1993

Speich, J. E., and Rosen, J., *Encyclopedia of Biomaterials and Biomedical Engineering*, University of California at Santa Cruz, 2004.

Sprague, Laurie A. et al., "Virtural Reality In Medical Education and Assessment", *Technology 2003*, December 2003.

Stauth, David, "Artificial Intelligence Systems More Apt to Fail Than to Destroy," *Phys.org*, March 24, 2015

Steenhuysen, Julie, "U.S. Biotech to Apply Artificial Intelligence to UK Genome Study," *Reuters*, September 30, 2015.

Stix, Gary, "Turn It Up, Dear," *Scientific American*, May 1, 2009.

Stonier, T, *Beyond Information: The Natural History of Intelligence*, Springer-Verlag, 1992.

Storm, Darlene, "Hello Kitty Hack Exposes 3.3 Million Users," *Computerworld*, December 22, 2015.

Tong, Christopher, *Artificial Intelligence in Engineering Design*, Elsevier, 2012.

Vardi, Moshe Y., *A Brief History of Logic*, 2003.

Vinge, Vernor, *The Coming Technological Singularity*, Vision-21, NASA, 1993.

Vlassis, Nikos, *A Concise Introduction to Multiagent Systems and Distributed Artificial Intelligence*, Morgan and Claypool, 2005.

Wagner, Meg, "Danger, Will Robinson: Don't Have Sex with Robots," *New York Daily News*, September 16, 2015.

Walsh, Toby, "Artificial Intelligence Should Benefit Society, Not Create Threats," *The Conversation*, January 16, 2015.

Wang, Joseph and Manesh, Kalayil, "Motion Control at the Nanoscale," *Small*, February 5, 2010.

Wolchover, Natalie, "Concerns of an Artificial Intelligence Pioneer," *Quanta*, April 21, 2015.

Worrall, Simon, "How Artificial Intelligence Will Revolutionize Our Lives," *National Geographic*, October 7, 2015.

Yudkowsky, Eliezer, et al., *Reducing Long Term Catastrophic Risks from Artificial Intelligence*, Machine Intelligence Research Institute, 2010.

Zadeh, L., *Fuzzy Sets and Fuzzy Logic*, World Scientific Publishing, 1996.

Zimmer, Carl, "Can You Live Forever?" *Scientific American*, December 22, 2010.

INDEX

THE LIFE SCIENCE INSTITUTE

The Life Science Institute is a global resource for practical and theoretical research, education, and information dissemination on scientific, economic, and social issues affecting the quality, perseverance, and future of civilization.

LifeScienceInstitute.com

About the Author

Dennis L. Foster is a renowned computer scientist, consultant, author, artist, explorer, and educator, known for his groundbreaking work in the development of artificial intelligence (AI) in the fields of educational technology, medical diagnosis, and robotics. Actively involved in AI research, software development, and implementation since the 1970s, he is the author of over 60 published books on a wide range of subjects, including AI, computers and programming, business management, finance, health care, sociology, education, behavior science, and marketing. The deployment and spread of his authored autotutorial learning systems via more than 18,000 universities, colleges, and technical schools since the early 1980s was the first global implementation of AI in education and a milestone in the real-world application of behavioral science learning technology.

He is the author of two best selling nonfiction books and seven featured book club selections devoted to innovation in technology. His books about AI and computer applications have been translated into seven languages, and his research has been cited by the United Nations.

He currently serves as CEO of Mundus Education Corporation and is also the volunteer Director of The Life Science Institute. He authors *The AI Insider* blog covering the influence of artificial intelligence on society, business, and work.